Getting the Buggers into Drama

Also available from Continuum

Learning to Teach Drama 11–18 2nd Edition – Andy Kempe and Helen Nicholson
Teaching Drama – Helen Nicholson
100 Ideas for Teaching Drama – Johnnie Young

Other titles by Sue Cowley:

Getting the Buggers to Behave 3rd Ed
Getting the Buggers to Think 2nd Ed
Getting the Buggers to Write 2nd Ed
How to Survive your First Year in Teaching
Guerilla Guide to Teaching 2nd Ed
Sue Cowley's Teaching Clinic
Sue Cowley's A–Z of Teaching
Getting your Little Darlings to Behave
Letting the Buggers be Creative

Getting the Buggers into Drama

SUE COWLEY

continuum

Continuum International Publishing Group

The Tower Building   80 Maiden Lane, Suite 704
11 York Road   New York, NY 10038
London SE1 7NX

www.continuumbooks.com

© Sue Cowley 2007

British Library Cataloguing-in-Publication Data
A catalogue record for this book is available from the British Library.

ISBN: 978–08264–9758–1 (paperback)

Cowley, Sue.
    Getting the buggers into drama : a practical guide to teaching drama / Sue Cowley.
    p. cm.
    Includes bibliographical references and index.
    ISBN–13: 978–0–8264–9758–1 (pbk. : alk. paper)
    ISBN–10: 0–8264–9758–6 (pbk. : alk. paper) 1. Drama – Study and teaching (Elementary) I. Title.
    PN1701.C69 2007
    372.66044 – dc22

2007021956

Typeset by Servis Filmsetting Ltd, Manchester
Printed and bound in Great Britain by Biddles Ltd.,
King's Lynn, Norfolk.

For John Rust-Andrews, who first showed me
how to get the buggers into drama

Contents

Contents

Contents

Acknowledgements

Thanks to all the teachers, performers, lecturers and others who over the years have shown me how to teach drama. Special thanks go to my mentor and friend, John Rust-Andrews.

Thanks to all the team at Continuum, especially my editor Alexandra Webster and marketing guru Mike Green.

And special thanks to Tilak, Álvie and Edite, for everything they do for me.

Introduction

Right from the earliest age, drama seems to strike a chord deep within us. Even before they begin school, children love to take on characters, to make up stories, and to role play using the simplest toys and objects. So it is that a cardboard box is turned into a barn for some toy animals, or a tea set and some play food are used to make a picnic for mum and dad to enjoy.

Once they begin their formal education, it seems there are fewer and fewer chances for children to live in the world of the imagination. In an increasingly crowded and target-driven curriculum, drama is often forced to take a back seat. Of course, we would all claim that 'our' subject is the one that should take centre stage, and that a particular area of the curriculum is the perfect one for engaging children and teaching them about the world; to my mind, though, drama really does offer the perfect format for so many kinds of learning. It teaches children about different perspectives, it shows them how to have empathy, it helps them to learn in a creative and exciting way. Drama can also help children build the vital skills of concentration, cooperation, confidence and consideration, alongside many others.

Drama in schools is of course about much more than teaching children how to stand up in the classroom or on stage and perform. Even for those children who would never dream of appearing in the school play, drama has numerous benefits that can feed into all other areas of the curriculum. Through imaginative activities, your students can encounter different cultures and societies, 'live' in different times and experience the full range of roles, occupations, and lifestyles that exist in the outside world. They can also learn how to work together, how to focus, and how to build a bond of trust with each other.

My aim in this book is to do two things. First, I want to give you an overview of the practicalities of using drama with young people. This book will show you how to manage your students, your teaching space and your resources to make the most of the drama work you do. It will also give you plenty of tips and ideas for staging a school production – to show the rest of the school and also the parents and the local community just how brilliant and exciting drama can be. Second, this book will give you hundreds of ideas for games, exercises, activities, scenarios and themes for teaching drama in your school. These are all explained in a straightforward, realistic and practical way. Hopefully you will be able to find many ideas here that are ideally suited to your individual situation.

My hope is that this book will help two very different kinds of teachers. I hope it will help those teachers who simply want to incorporate a bit more imaginative activity into their classrooms. Perhaps you are a primary teacher unsure of just how you might make use of drama; or a secondary teacher in a subject other than drama, who wishes to engage your students through using dramatic approaches? If so, this book is for you. I also hope this book will help those teachers who already have some knowledge of or experience in teaching drama, and who are looking for some new ideas to try.

Above all else, I do hope you enjoy reading this book as much as I've enjoyed writing it. And of course I also hope that you enjoy teaching the drama activities given here to your students. Drama has played a key role throughout my life. The opportunity to pass my love of it on to others is both a pleasure and a privilege.

Sue Cowley
www.suecowley.co.uk

- your experience of teaching the subject
- the topic you are exploring
- the skills you are teaching
- whether you are teaching drama as a discrete subject or as a way of delivering another part of the curriculum.

However, a typical one-hour lesson might look something like this:

- individual warm-up – perhaps moving around the space in different ways
- whole class warm up – the class come together for a group activity
- whole-class discussion – introducing and brainstorming on the topic
- small group improvisations – the teacher gives some parameters and then sets off a series of planned or unplanned improvisations
- whole-class improvisation – using the same topic, the whole class does a 'tag improvisation' where the students move in and out of the scene in turn
- a cool-down – the teacher uses a relaxation exercise to bring the children 'back down' before they leave for their next lesson.

Classroom management for drama

Drama is an artistic subject, one in which much value is put on imagination and free expression. It takes place in a space where the children have freedom of movement, where they are unconstrained by desks and chairs. Although some written work will be necessary, there is much less focus on this than in many other subjects. Looking at actors on the television and in the cinema, your students may have gained the (very much mistaken) impression that drama is an 'easy way' to fame and fortune, and that it requires little technical skill. This means that your children might approach drama sessions with certain preconceptions about how they should work and behave.

The effective actor has very high levels of self-discipline. When working as part of a group, particularly in live theatre, the demands for discipline and focus are even higher. The fact that acting 'looks' easy is about high levels of technique and skill, rather than the opposite.

As a teacher of drama, you need to put very clear structures and routines in place. This will free up your children to give rein to their creative and imaginative talents. It's worth remembering that, as a physical subject, there will be health and safety issues in a drama lesson. Having clear rules and a good handle on behaviour will help you to create a safe, effective climate for drama.

Here are some tips about classroom management, based on my own experiences of teaching drama, and on good practice that I have seen from other drama teachers.

- *Set the standards from the start:* Use your first few sessions for creating a clear and unswerving set of expectations about how the students will behave. Get them trained up quickly in your ways of working, so that they can get on with the fun stuff of actually doing drama.
- *Have an entry routine:* Set up an unchanging routine for what the students do when they arrive at drama. You will of course need to adapt this routine, depending on the kind of space you have for your drama sessions. Here is an 'ideal' model.
  o The students line up outside the room.
  o The teacher allows them in one by one, checking for gum, jewellery, etc.
  o Immediately after entering, the students take off their shoes.
  o Bags, coats and shoes are placed in an allocated area.
  o Once this is done, the students form a circle, seated on the floor.
  o When all the students are ready, the teacher sits with them.
  o This is the signal for silence, and for the lesson to begin.
- *Decide how you will deal with a non-studio space:* Sometimes you may have to teach drama in a traditional classroom. If this is the case, make clear decisions ahead of time about how you are going to create a space for the drama work. My advice would be to involve the children in moving chairs and desks to the

sides of the room and back again at the end, spending time on getting this right in the first few lessons.

- *Have a clear set of rules:* Just as in any normal classroom, you need to communicate your rules to the children. This will be done in the first few lessons, and also you might create some posters to put around the room, so that you can refer back to what is expected. When planning your rules, consider safety a priority – just like PE, the physical nature of drama makes this vital. For example, you might think about some or all of the following, in addition to your normal school rules.
  o Shoes off and any gum in the bin.
  o Jewellery, especially big earrings, to be taken off.
  o Students to wear loose, comfy clothes (you may or may not feel that changing for drama is necessary).
  o Stop work immediately if the teacher asks.
  o Listen, in complete silence, when someone is talking to the class.
  o Show respect to other students, the teacher and the space.
  o Take an active part in the lesson.
- *Use a circle as a control mechanism:* A whole class circle, with the teacher included, offers a great way of starting off lessons. It is very useful for when you wish to speak to the class together, or when you want to discuss ideas with the group as a whole. There are also a large number of drama exercises that you can do using this format. The circle offers a wonderfully democratic structure that works particularly well in drama lessons.
- *Have a stop signal:* Because drama is often a noisy subject, it's particularly important for the teacher to agree a stop signal with the class, i.e. 'when you see me do this, you must stop, look and listen'. That way you won't have to shout over the noise of 30 excited children every time you need to speak to the class.
- *Practise your stop signal:* Spend plenty of time practising with the students, so that they respond instantly to the agreed signal. You might use this as a warm-up in your first few lessons with a class.
- *Change your stop signal regularly:* In my experience, after a while, stop signals begin to lose their effectiveness. It's therefore wise to instigate a new stop signal from time to time. For instance:

9

○ The teacher puts a hand up, then all students must do the same.
○ A noise sounds such as a bell or five claps.
○ The teacher sits, all students must sit in silence.
○ A visual signal is made, such as switching off the class lights or switching on a set of fairy lights.

Drama spaces

Drama is taught in a whole host of different spaces. In some secondary schools, particularly those with an expressive arts specialism, it has its own dedicated drama studio or theatre. If you're really lucky, this could be equipped with blackout blinds, a sound system, lights, a lighting board and a separate area for costumes and props. There might even be a technician on site who is able to help with setting up lights, sound equipment, etc. In other secondary schools, and in many primaries, there are very few resources and drama is done in a classroom with the furniture moved to one side, or in the school hall.

Often, it takes an inspirational head of drama to push the profile of the subject and get the ball rolling. If you are currently teaching in an inadequate space, you might need to fight for several years to get the studio space and other resources you require. Having a dedicated drama space will have huge benefits in terms of what can go on in lessons. It also puts both teacher and children in the right frame of mind for serious drama.

If you have a great space, I'm sure you are already making the most of it. If you're stuck with a classroom or other inadequate area for drama, here are some tips born of my own experience of teaching in a non-studio space.

– *Moving furniture:* Spend the first few lessons 'training up' your students in how to move the furniture efficiently. Find lots of ways to make this feel like a valid part of the lesson, by setting targets and offering rewards when it is done well. Be firm – if it's not done properly then get the class to do it again. With a class of around 30 students, and some proper teamwork and delegation, clearing a classroom of furniture should not take more than a couple of minutes. Make sure that you leave slightly more time at the end of the lesson to get the classroom back to how it was (the motivation for clearing up is never as strong as the urge to get started).

- *Getting the students in the right frame of mind:* It's inevitable that drama in a classroom will 'feel' different to drama in a proper performance space. As a result, you need to make even more effort to create an atmosphere if you're working in a classroom. Make plenty of use of costumes, props, music and so on. See the section on 'Creating atmosphere' (p. 65–7) for more ideas.

- *Managing the students within the space:* Where a classroom is being used for drama, it's often the case that there is not really enough space for the students to work efficiently. Here are some suggestions for making the most of a small space.

  o Do lots of activities with the whole class in a circle – as structures go, a circle offers the best format for maximizing a space and involving all the students.

  o When you divide the class into groups, find a way to clarify the area where each group should work. This might involve chairs, masking tape, whatever comes to hand. Be strict about students sticking to their own group's space.

  o Use activities such as tag improvisations (see p. 32–3), where all the students can take part, but not necessarily all at the same time.

  o When improvising, consider splitting the class into two, with one half watching the other half perform. This will make good use of space and mean that the students don't spend too much time sitting watching each other.

  o In lessons where the thought of moving the furniture just doesn't appeal, explore some aspects of theatre that don't involve performance. For instance, get the students to make some papier mâché masks or to create some three-dimensional set designs.

- *Dealing with the wide open space:* Sometimes, the problem is not with a cramped classroom but with the opposite, a huge open space such as a hall or canteen. This does have its benefits: there's a lovely feeling of freedom and you probably won't

11

have to waste lesson time clearing furniture. Unfortunately, there are several downsides, including issues with noise and sometimes with student behaviour. If you have to teach drama in a wide open space, try the following strategies for maintaining focus and control.

o Have an agreed 'silence signal' to get the class's attention, and insist that the students practise responding quickly to it. Consider whether it is best to use a sound or a visual signal (this will depend on the space that you're in). At all costs, avoid shouting to get the children's attention, as this will only add to the overall noise levels.

o Encourage the students to be aware of their own noise levels, and get them to practise talking at different volumes. Be conscious of the acoustics in the space – if the room is very echoey, make an effort to use a very low volume when you address the class.

o Be firm about your standards from the start. If possible, line the class up outside the space before they enter to clarify your expectations. Use a circle to begin every lesson, and sanction any children who run around the room rather than going straight to sit down.

2

Ways of working

In this chapter, I look at the different ways of working that might be used during a drama lesson, giving you a definition of the various terms that you will come across in this book, and examples of each way of working. I also include a brief rundown of the pros and cons of using each method, and some tips for getting the best out of your students. This chapter will be especially useful for those new to teaching the subject, and it can also act as a reference and a reminder to more experienced staff.

Individual focus

The students sit or stand, usually with their eyes shut. They are asked to use their imagination/concentration in various ways, for instance to think about a character, to listen for sounds, to go on an imaginative journey, and so on.

For an example, see p. 35.

Pros

- This is an excellent way to start a lesson.
- It helps the students learn how to concentrate.
- It's great for calming a lively class.

- A focus will help you bring the children 'into' the lesson/space and help them put aside any distractions from previous lessons.
- An individual focus can be done in a circle, a group or in a space.

Cons

- Some children may 'opt out', sitting with eyes shut but brains disconnected.
- Some students may refuse to close their eyes.
- At first, students may feel embarrassed and there may be some silly behaviour.

Top tips

- When you start using this approach, sit each child in an individual space, as far away from others as possible. Ask them to turn so that they are facing away from other students. This should minimize the potential for distraction.
- Tell the class: 'You have your eyes shut, I have mine open, so I can check!' If a student has his or her eyes open, it's better to give them a deadly stare than to draw attention to the individual's behaviour.

Warm-ups

These are exercises that get the children physically, vocally and mentally prepared for a drama lesson. These exercises can be used at the start of the lesson, and also before a rehearsal for a show. The children might warm up their bodies, their voices, or focus on a particular skill.

For lots of examples, see Chapters 3 and 4.

Pros

- These are great as a starter activity for a drama lesson, especially where the class is fidgety and keen to get moving.

- For lessons that will involve lots of physical activity, warm-ups are essential for avoiding injury. They are as vital in drama as in PE or dance.
- A vocal warm-up is important if the students are going to be doing a lot of voice work.
- Many warm-ups offer a good way of getting the children to work together and to learn how to cooperate.

Cons

- Some students view warm-ups as games, rather than as a serious part of the work, and consequently refuse to take them as seriously.
- With the more active exercises, you will need to watch out for silly or dangerous behaviour, and know what you are going to do to counter it.
- Take care that there isn't a long gap between the warm-up and the rest of the lesson, while you are explaining the work. This of course negates the whole purpose of the warm-up, which is to get and stay warm.

Top tips

- Talk with the class about why it's necessary to warm up for drama. Encourage them to see the subject as a physical, technical subject, as well as a creative and artistic one.
- Make a warm-up part of your regular routine, perhaps interspersing it as a starter with the individual focus exercises described above.

Trust games

These are activities that rely on the children's ability to trust their fellow students, and also to be trustworthy. Trust games encourage (indeed, force) the children to work together and cooperate. In order for the activity to 'work', the children must take care of each other, rather than trying to catch each other out. Many trust

15

games involve the students closing their eyes and relying on a partner.

For an example, see p. 40.

Pros

- The students learn cooperation and consideration, two skills that are vital for drama and particularly important for effective group performances.
- They also learn that it is okay to put their faith and trust in each other. For those children from difficult backgrounds, who are used to being let down, this can be a very valuable life lesson to learn.
- Trust games and exercises can be a lot of fun.

Cons

- Some students will inevitably let you and their classmates down, by refusing to behave in a trustworthy way. This is frustrating and disappointing for both the teacher and the children.
- If the students' behaviour is very poor, trust games can be potentially dangerous. It can be tricky to find a balance between putting your faith in your children and the need to avoid excessive risks.
- For some students it is easy enough to be trustworthy in a simple game, but harder to transfer their new-found cooperative skills to a performance.

Top tips

- Make it clear that anyone who behaves in a dangerous way will be asked to sit out from the activity.
- Try a 'drip feed' approach, starting with simple exercises that cannot go too far wrong if the children do not cooperate. Gradually introduce activities that ask for higher levels of cooperation.

- Act as a role model – take part in demonstrating the exercises yourself. Show the students that you are happy to put your trust in others, and they will be more likely to do the same.

Pairwork

A lot of short drama exercises are done with the students working with a partner, particularly skills-based exercises at the beginning of the lesson. With only two people involved, pairwork is straightforward and an ideal format for developing characterization techniques.

For an example, see p. 46.

Pros

- Pairwork takes away some of the pressure of working on your own, but without the added complications of being in a group.
- With only two students working together, it's easier for them to cooperate. For instance, there is less chance that the students will talk over each other during a performance.
- It's quick and easy to organize; it's as simple as saying 'find a partner'.

Cons

- Where students end up working with a friend, they can sometimes find it hard to take the activity as seriously as they should.
- Where a student is asked to work with one other person, if there are tensions between the two of them this can cause friction. Of course, it's also potentially a great opportunity to build bridges.

Top tips

- Because working in pairs happens so frequently in the typical drama lesson, and because it is often used just for a quick

activity, you might sometimes allow the students to choose their own partners.
- Make it clear that you are doing this on purpose, perhaps as a reward for good behaviour, and that it should be viewed as a special treat.
- For a random method of getting into pairs, ask the students to pair up with the person standing closest to them.

Small group work

A great number of drama activities take place in a small group format, so it really is worth getting it exactly right in order to offer the best possible learning opportunity. There are a range of exercises that could be done in a small group, such as an unplanned improvisation or a scripted performance.

For an example, see p. 117.

Pros

- Groups of about four to six students provide the perfect environment for planned and unplanned improvisations.
- There are enough people to offer plenty of ideas, but not too many for an effective group discussion to take place.
- There are also enough people to play a range of different characters, but not so many that the performance becomes confused or confusing.

Cons

- Some students find it hard to handle groupwork, and for instance have trouble sharing ideas, working cooperatively, and so on. This is a skill that they need to learn, and the best way to learn it is through practice.
- Where friendships are allowed to dictate the groupings for drama, this can lead to an overly relaxed learning environment, where there is too much social chat and off-task behaviour.

- When tensions arise within a class, it can be tricky to persuade certain students to work together.
- Some of the less socially adept children can be difficult to 'place' within a group. Students are not always terribly subtle about making their feelings known about those they are asked to work with.

Top tips

- Make it clear from the very first lesson that the students must be willing to work with anybody and everybody. Insist on respectful attitudes and clamp down immediately on anyone who is rude or who says 'I can't work with . . .'.
- Insist that the students learn to be 'professionals'; that they put aside any problems or tensions from outside the lesson and just get on with the work.
- Use random methods to create groups, in order to avoid the difficulties created by friendship groups. Here's one good way to do this.
  o Sit or stand the whole class in a circle.
  o Divide the number in the class by the number required in each group (e.g. 25 students, 5 in a group = 5).
  o With odd numbers, don't worry about the 'extra' children – you can simply have a couple of groups with one extra person.
  o Get the students to count out loud around the circle to obtain 'their' number (i.e. 1, 2, 3, 4, 5 . . . 1, 2, 3, 4, 5).
  o Ask the children with each number to raise a hand, so that the students know who they are working with and cannot mix up the groups either inadvertently or deliberately.
  o Allocate an area of the drama space to each group.
  o Allow the numbered groups to go to their space one group at a time, starting with one and moving upwards. This will help you ensure that the students go into the correct group.

Improvisation

Improvisation is effectively 'making it up as you go along'. This technique allows the children to experience 'being' someone else, in a different situation, without necessarily having to create a finished performance. The technique effectively falls into two types, the planned and unplanned improvisation. In a planned improvisation, the students first discuss the characters they will play and what these characters are going to do, before going into the improvisation. An unplanned improvisation is exactly that – the teacher gives a setting, scenario or some characters, and the students immediately begin to act.

For an example, see p. 93.

Pros

- Drama in schools is about more than just watching a finished performance: improvisation provides a welcome antidote to lessons full of show and tell, which can be very dull for the audience.
- All the children in the class can improvise simultaneously – it allows everyone to take part at their own level of confidence or interest.
- Improvisation teaches the children how to empathize with and understand other people's thoughts and feelings.
- When the children take part in and evaluate improvisations, they develop their drama skills and their understanding of dramatic techniques. For instance, they might be looking at building a more realistic character or using dramatic tension more effectively.

Cons

- Those students who do not really engage with the subject will often improvise in a childish, superficial way.
- With a less experienced, younger or immature class, you might find that you get more play fights in the scenes than is absolutely necessary.

- Although unplanned improvisations are great for keeping things moving in a lesson, if you use too many of them they can end up seeming rather throw-away and lacking in depth.

Top tips

- When students choose to opt out by producing silly or unrealistic improvisations, I've found it is best to ignore them rather than make an issue of it. Focus on what your 'good' students are doing instead.
- Use a good balance of planned and unplanned improvisations. Think of the unplanned improvisation as a good starter or warm-up exercise. Then move on to a planned improvisation to allow the students to explore the characters/situation in more depth.
- Improvisations work best with plenty of dramatic tension. The teacher can provide this by giving a reason for tension: for example, an argument or the build-up to an important event.

Freeze-frames

The students create a frozen picture that captures a moment. This might be done individually, in pairs, in groups, or as a whole class. The freeze-frame can be used for many things: for instance, it might sum up a topic or emotion, capture an event in a story or summarise a story.

For an example, see p. 154.

Pros

- The freeze-frame is quick and simple to arrange. It need not take the students more than a couple of minutes to organize.
- It is a great way of summarizing a topic or of focusing on a specific moment during a scene.
- Because the picture is frozen, it's ideal for getting the rest of the class to look at and think about it in detail.

- Using freeze-frames is a great way to encourage focus from your students – they must freeze completely still and hold the position for a period of time.

Cons

- Because of its simplicity, sometimes a freeze-frame can be dashed off by the students without too much proper thought.
- Some students might find it hard to stay frozen, becoming giggly and fidgety, particularly when the rest of the class is watching.
- If you use this technique a lot, it can become a bit 'same-y' and uninspiring for the students. See the ideas below for some more creative ways of using a freeze.

Top tips

- Give the group or class a 'moment' when they will all be standing frozen. Say '3, 2, 1, freeze', at which point the students should all freeze.
- Where your students are a bit giggly, set a time target to encourage their total focus. Start with a short time – say about ten seconds – then gradually increase this as the students' focus improves.
- Play around with the freeze-frames you use, for instance you could:
  o Look at the ten seconds before or after the frozen moment.
  o Unfreeze the picture and continue in slow motion.
  o 'Rewind' the image, going backwards.
  o Use a series of freeze-frames to summarize scenes in a story.

Hot seating

A student sits in a chair which is known as the 'hot seat'. This person is then questioned, as a character, by the other students. Hot seating can be adapted for a range of purposes, but is typically used to find out more about a character. For instance, it might be used to encourage the students to think about characterization, or to delve into a character's motivations. Hot seating has lots of links to English and can be used to help a class to study a character from a novel or play in more detail.

For an example, see p. 167–8.

Pros

- Being put 'on the spot' forces the student in the hot seat to think on his or her feet and to be flexible and inventive.
- The student in the hot seat will often come up with very creative and imaginative ideas about the person they are playing.
- The exercise can help to deepen the students' knowledge of a book or play.
- It's simple to set up and do, and can easily take place in a classroom if there is no drama space available.

Cons

- Going in the hot seat requires a fair bit of confidence, because it's effectively like taking the stage on your own. Sometimes it can be hard to persuade the students to take part.
- Where hot seating is used to study a fictional character, the student in the hot seat needs to know enough about the person they are portraying. If they do not, they can end up giving answers that are inaccurate and potentially confusing.
- At first the questions that the class asks of the character may seem rather superficial. Given time, though, the students will usually begin to delve deeper.

Top tips

- If the students are not fully familiar with a fictional character you are studying, or if they are a bit uncertain about doing the activity, consider taking the hot seat yourself. This will encourage them to participate.

- Consider giving the rest of the class a role as well, so that they question the student in the hot seat in character.

Judgement chair

This technique is similar to hot seating, with a volunteer sat in the 'judgement chair' playing a specific character. In this instance, though, the people coming up to the chair are also in character and are there to pass judgement on the person. The student in the chair can talk back to those judging them, perhaps giving reasons for the behaviour, or alternatively decide to stay silent.

This exercise is great for getting the children thinking about a range of perspectives. It is also very valuable for looking at moral issues, and at how we should try to respect other people's views. So, a bully might sit in the judgement chair, and various characters (the victim, her parents, a teacher, a social worker) come up and say what they think.

For an example, see p. 108.

Pros

- This exercise gives children a deeper insight into many different moral issues. It shows them that there is not necessarily one 'right' answer or way of thinking.
- The judgement chair encourages the students to feel empathy – to see that their own behaviour can seriously affect a range of other people.

Cons

- At first, the students can find it hard to understand the difference between this and hot seating, and might be a bit reluctant to take part.
- For the person in the judgement chair, this can be quite a difficult and emotional experience, so you will need to choose your volunteers with care.

Top tips

- If the students are slow to get going, show them what a couple of different characters might say by going up to pass judgement yourself.
- With older students you might develop the technique by staging a fully fledged courtroom scene, with lawyers, witnesses, etc.

Thought tracking

A character's inner thoughts are spoken out loud, giving us access to their feelings, motivations, hopes, fears, etc. A thought track might take place during a frozen moment in a scene, or perhaps be performed as a monologue.

For an example, see p. 154.

Pros

- This exercise encourages the students to see that realistic characterization is about knowing the person from the inside out.
- Thought tracking encourages children to deepen and develop the characters that they portray.
- Thought tracking connects to the 'method acting' approach – to the idea that you have to become a character in order to portray a character accurately, experiencing what that person experiences.

Cons

- The exercise can be done in a rather superficial way, with the student saying what they think you want to hear, rather than what the character might actually say.
- For those students who do not take drama seriously as a subject, this can seem like an odd thing to do, and it can be difficult for them not to laugh.

Top tips

- Thought tracking works well during a whole-class improvisation. 'Freeze' the scene then move around tapping individuals on the shoulder to ask them to voice their thoughts.
- You don't always need to plan a thought track into the lesson. You can also use it in a spontaneous way, when you see that a student or character might be turning something over in his or her mind.

Conscience alley / Thought tunnel

The conscience alley or thought tunnel has a similar effect to thought tracking, but on a grander and often more deeply affecting scale. The students make two lines, facing inwards, about the width of a person apart. This creates an 'alleyway' down the centre of the room. A volunteer walks down the middle of the tunnel, preferably with his or her eyes shut to heighten the effect. As the person passes them, the students give comments or make sounds, depending on the focus you are using. In most instances the students should not touch the person walking down the alley. (You might change this if you are doing something like 'walking through a spooky forest' and you trust the children to be gentle.)

For an example, see p. 169.

Pros

- This exercise is great for getting inside the head of a character, and considering that person's motivation.
- It also works very effectively for creating an atmosphere and looking at how sound effects can work.
- The whole class has to take part for the activity to work fully, so it's great for encouraging participation and cooperation.

Cons

- It can take longer than you might think to actually get the students to create a straight alleyway the right distance apart.
- Sometimes the temptation to reach out and touch the person walking down the alley can be too much.
- At first you might find that the students over play it, making loud noises to try and surprise the person, rather than quieter ones which are more effective.

Top tips

- Try using the alley to look at two sides of an issue, with each side of the tunnel representing a different perspective. For instance, when looking at bullying, as the bully walks down the tunnel, one side could be the victim's thoughts, the other side could be the bully's.
- Leave plenty of time for this activity. Once you get started, you will find that most or all of the children want to have a go.
- Encourage the students to make a sound only as the person actually passes by them. Often, the quieter the words or sound effects, the more effective the alleyway exercise will be.
- After they have walked down the alley, ask the students for a few comments about how the experience felt. Encourage them to evaluate what the rest of the class have achieved during the activity, and how they might improve.

The role of the expert

With this technique, the students take on the role of an 'expert' in a particular subject. So, they might be police detectives, government scientists, doctors, architects and so on. Working in this role, they are asked to solve problems and create improvised stories. The technique is effectively an extension of the role plays that children do when they are young.

For an example, see p. 168–9.

Pros

- Once they get into character, the children often treat the work with great seriousness. Taking on the role seems to encourage them to adopt more mature and adult attitudes.
- The teacher can use the role to remind the students of how they must behave, i.e. an expert or professional would do this/wouldn't do that.
- The problem-solving done during this activity is very engaging for the students. There are very rarely any classroom management issues when you are using the role of the expert.
- This technique encourages creative and lateral thinking in response to the problems that need solving.
- The students respond really well to the 'real life' nature of this exercise – they are playing real people in potentially real situations.

Cons

- To be technically accurate in the portrayal, the children need a reasonable idea of what their expert actually does.
- With younger students, a lack of knowledge can lead to some rather superficial or stereotyped characterizations.

Top tips

- If your students do not have a great deal of background knowledge about what a particular character does, get them to do some research as a homework task.
- If you can incorporate props and costumes into the mix, this can add a great deal to the students' engagement with the exercise.
- If the drama starts to go a bit flat, throw another (bigger, more insoluble) problem at your experts.

Whole-class improvisation

The students work together, in role, to create a piece of drama. The drama is typically based on a situation or setting given by the teacher. A whole-class improvisation might be used at the end of a topic, bringing together everything that the students have learned. Alternatively, it can also be used as a format through which an entire topic is explored, both in drama and also in other subjects. For this technique to work properly, all the students need to be willing to participate and cooperate, staying focused and in character.

For an example, see p. 154–5.

Pros

- When a whole-class improvisation really comes off, it can be one of the most powerful and moving drama techniques of all.
- This activity can create a wonderful sense of community, of the class creating a piece of theatre together.
- Whole-class improvisation can be used across the curriculum, in the classroom as well as in the drama studio.
- Approaching a topic by *being* a character (e.g. a medieval peasant) will give the children greater insight into how these people felt and behaved.
- The children typically find this approach very engaging, exciting and inspirational.

Cons

- This is a difficult technique and it can take quite a bit of time before a class is able to pull it off.
- If the class do get overexcited, or start to mess around, you might need to stop the activity to refocus them.
- It can be hard to plan the timing of a lesson involving a whole-class improvisation – if it's not working, you might need to stop it early, so have some back-up ideas for other activities.

Top tips

- You will need to build up slowly to a whole-class improvisation, particularly with children who have not done much drama before.

- Take on a role yourself, within the drama, as this will help you manage the students without breaking the 'spell' of the story.
- Don't be afraid to 'freeze' the improvisation and step in as required, perhaps to refocus the class or to add a twist to the storyline.

Teacher in role

During a piece of whole-class drama (as above), the teacher takes on a character inside the story. The teacher then uses this character to direct or develop the drama. For example, the teacher might enter the room with a clipboard, claiming to be a government scientist and explaining to the students that there are only 24 hours left before an asteroid hits the Earth. The teacher could then guide the students into holding a meeting to decide what should be done.

For an example, see p. 159.

Pros

- Playing a part inside the drama gives you greater control over the progress and direction of the story.
- There is no need to freeze the story and come out of character to talk with the class; this helps you avoid breaking the imaginative 'spell' that can take hold of the class.
- You can encourage the students to deepen their characterization by asking questions or giving suggestions in character.
- The children typically love to see their teacher getting involved in the lesson. It inspires and motivates them to join in too.

Cons

- It can be tempting to take too much control of the direction of the drama – make sure you allow the students to play a part in the decision-making process as well.
- Sometimes the children can lose their concentration because they find it so amusing to see their teacher playing a role.

- In all honesty, it can sometimes feel a bit silly to use teacher in role. You will need to overcome any reticence on your part and remember how it felt to be a kid.

Top tips

- When using this technique, it can work very well to start the lesson with a 'bang', by going straight into character without any explanation.
- If the students are not working properly, or if they don't quite understand what to do, you might need to drop out of role for a moment to talk with them.
- It's often best to take on a character that naturally has a leadership role. That way you can stay in charge without dropping in and out of role too often.
- If you have a very talented or confident student in your class, you might like to hand over the main role to this person and see what happens.

Meetings

Meetings are very useful as a format for drama and discussion work. They can be used within a drama lesson, and also in a situation where the teacher wishes to do some in-role work in a classroom, without needing to move furniture around. During a meeting, the teacher and students might be given or take on roles, depending on the scenario. Meetings could be staged as a whole-class improvisation, or working in smaller groups.

For instance, you could use a small group meeting to discuss a child's progress at school, with the students being allocated the roles of teachers, social workers, form tutor, welfare officer, etc. For older students, 'meeting' formats such as a séance or a rehab group can lead to some very intense, thought-provoking and interesting drama.

For an example, see p. 161–2.

31

Pros

- This is a real-life structure that can be applied to many different topics.
- The students are encouraged to take on a range of realistic characters from within the drama.
- Meetings are particularly useful for issues-based work, where strong viewpoints and opinions can be expressed.
- The students learn how to present an argument and back it up with evidence, a skill that is very useful in essay writing and in subjects across the curriculum.

Cons

- Some children will take a back seat and allow others to dominate the discussion.
- It can be hard to plan the timing of a lesson in which the meeting format is used – sometimes the meeting will be over quite quickly, at other times it will progress really well and it can seem a shame to cut it short.

Top tips

- Take on a role that allows you to elicit contributions from the quieter, less forthcoming students. For instance, you could be the chairperson in a council meeting.
- Choose the more confident and able students to play roles on the panel, as they are more likely to be responsive and flexible.

Tag improvisation

A scene is set (a park, a hotel lobby) and three or four students are put into the story. They go straight into an unplanned improvisation based in that location, developing their characters as they go along. As one student leaves the scene, another volunteer is 'tagged' and can enter the story. The rest of the class watch the improvisation as they wait to take part.

For an example, see p. 147.

Pros

- This is a great exercise for getting the students to think on their feet and to be creative and imaginative within an improvisation.
- It's a good compromise between a small group and whole-class improvisation. Although the whole class can take part, they are only doing so in a reasonably small number at any one time.
- The rest of the group acts as a kind of audience; watching others improvise (especially the more confident students) can be very instructive for your less able children.

Cons

- Some students might choose to opt out by not getting up to be tagged.
- For less confident children, having the whole class watching them do an unplanned improvisation can feel a bit frightening.
- Your more confident students might decide to stay in the scenario for rather longer than is necessary.
- Sometimes the characters that are used can be rather superficial or stereotyped.

Top tips

- If you have a class where some children always volunteer, and others opt out, make it a rule that each person can only come into the scenario once.
- Encourage your students to have a good reason as to why their character is entering or leaving the improvisation.
- Add props and furniture to the scene to make it more interesting and realistic.
- If the scene starts to falter or lose tension, enter yourself, in role, to add an interesting angle to the story.

3

Building drama skills

In order to create good quality drama, children need to build up a range of drama skills. As I've already explained, these skills are doubly useful because they transfer so well into learning in other subjects. Exercises designed to develop drama skills can be built into the lesson as a warm-up, a cool-down, or as part of a wider topic. They might also be used by teachers in other subjects as a starter activity or as a way of punctuating longer periods of concentrated effort.

Concentration

Concentration is one of the most essential skills needed for an effective performance, whether it's a simple improvisation in the classroom or a full-length play on a West End stage. Actors will often talk about a sense of 'focus' – a feeling of being completely immersed in the situation, in the character, in what is happening at that precise moment. There are strong similarities between this sense of focus and the idea of a working meditation.

Without a good focus, it is all too easy for an actor to drop out of character, to forget his or her lines, or to lose concentration and start laughing. Learning how to concentrate and focus is, to my mind, one of the most important things that drama can teach children. Ideally, they should be able to take these skills out of the drama setting and use them in other curriculum areas. Indeed, the ability to concentrate is a vital life skill that will go beyond the immediate school setting and into their everyday lives.

Focus exercises

Focus exercises are a great way of teaching your children how to concentrate more effectively. They work particularly well as a starter activity, to focus the students for the learning to come. I've split the ideas below into focus exercises that are done individually, in pairs, and as a whole class.

Individual focus exercises

Focused listening

- *Sit on your own in a space on the floor.*
- *Close your eyes.*
- *Listen carefully for any sounds. Start inside the room then move your focus to the corridor, then beyond.*
- *What did you hear?*
- *What does this exercise force you to do?*

Focused visualization

- *Sit on your own in a space on the floor.*
- *Picture yourself standing in the drama room.*
- *Mentally 'walk' around the room, looking at each part in turn.*
- *Now open your eyes and look around.*
- *What did this exercise ask you to do?*
- *How well could you visualize the room?*
- *Which details did you miss, and why?*

Walk and freeze

- *Stand on your own in a space in the room.*
- *Walk around the room, using all the space.*
- *When you hear the first drumbeat, freeze instantly.*

- *When you hear the second drumbeat, move off.*
- *Aim to move off with a sense of purpose, as though you are going somewhere.*
- *What are you concentrating on here?*
- *Why is this exercise relatively easy?*

Walk, freeze and turn

- *Now repeat the exercise, developing it further. This time:*
  - ○ *freeze on the first beat*
  - ○ *turn to face a different direction on the second*
  - ○ *move off on the third.*
- *Is this harder than before?*
- *If so, why has it become harder to do?*

Walk and freeze with counting

- Repeat the walking exercises above.
- This time, though, tell students: *At the same time as you walk, count backwards from 50 to zero in your head.*
- *Why has the exercise suddenly become very difficult?*

Walk at a distance

- Stand in a space.
- Choose one other person, without letting that person know that you have chosen them.
- Walk around the room.
- As you walk, keep exactly the same distance between you and the person you chose.
- *What skill are you using here?*
- *Why is it hard to focus on two things at one time?*
- *Why do you think this skill is important in drama?*

Walk in a triangle

- Stand in a space.
- Choose two other people, but again, do not let them know you have chosen them.

- *As you walk, form an equilateral triangle.*
- *If the people you have chosen move further apart, all three sides of the triangle must become bigger and vice versa.*
- *Is this harder than with one person?*
- *Why is it harder?*

Paired focus exercises

The stare

- *Face a partner.*
- *Stare into each other's eyes without laughing or blinking.*
- *If you break eye contact you are 'out' and you must both sit down.*
- *Why are you tempted to break eye contact?*
- *Have you ever done this to a stranger?*
- *Why is it different with someone you don't know?*

Mirrors

- *Stand facing a partner.*
- *Imagine there is a mirror in between you.*
- *With one person leading, mirror your partner's actions exactly (i.e. right arm/left arm).*
- *On the drumbeat, swap leaders.*
- Ask half the class to watch the other half.
- *Can you tell who is leading?*
- *If not, what does this mean about how well the exercise is being done?*

Hypnosis

- *Stand facing a partner.*
- *Use your hand, palm forwards, to 'hypnotize' the other person.*
- *Your partner should keep their face a few inches from the palm of your hand at all times.*
- *Move your partner around the room, up and down, etc.*
- *Change 'hypnotists' on the drumbeat.*

- *The aim is to move smoothly, rather than to catch your partner out.*
- Ask half the class to watch the other half.
- *Who is doing it best? Why have you picked these people as the 'best'?*

Cars

- *Stand behind your partner.*
- *You are going to 'drive' them with their eyes shut.*
- *The signals are:*
    o *both hands on small of back = go straight forwards*
    o *both hands on shoulders = brake*
    o *tap on right shoulder = quarter turn right*
    o *tap on left shoulder = quarter turn left.*
- *If you crash into another pair you must sit out.*
- *Do not force your partner to go faster than they want to.*
- *The object of the exercise is trust and focus, not speed.*

Whole-class focus exercises

Throw the ball

- *Stand as a whole class in a circle.*
- *Throw a ball around and across the circle.*
- *Make eye contact with the person before you throw.*
- *Do not drop the ball.*
- *Does making eye contact help you to catch the ball?*
- *Why does this help you?*

Throw the invisible ball

- *Now throw an invisible ball around/across the circle.*
- *Again, make eye contact with the person before you throw.*
- *The object of this exercise is realism.*
- *Are you really creating a ball or just waving your arms around?*
- *Is it harder with or without the ball?*

Walk without seeing

- Stand in a space on your own.
- Shut your eyes.
- Walk around the room with your eyes shut, without bumping into anyone.
- What do you have to do to make it work?
- What skills are you using here?
- This is hard, but not impossible, to do successfully.

Cooperation

You might find that your children, raised on a diet of Hollywood movie stars, believe that acting is very much an individual activity. At first, your students may find it hard to cooperate with anyone outside their normal friendship groupings. (This is one reason why it's so useful to insist right from the start in drama lessons that they do work with anyone and everyone.) Before you try the exercises given below, it's well worth doing some discussion about why cooperation is so important for doing drama.

With older students, you might like to look at the vocabulary around the idea of a group effort which crops up so repeatedly in drama. For instance:

- ensemble
- company
- chorus
- troupe
- cast
- unison.

It is also useful to introduce the term 'blocking' to the students. Blocking means a situation where one actor refuses to cooperate, putting up a metaphorical wall and blocking every suggestion that is made by the other performers. Where one person blocks the others, this can completely stifle an improvisation.

Cooperation exercises

The exercises below are all designed to encourage your students to cooperate more fully. Many of them would make a useful starter activity, although you could also devote an entire lesson to the idea of developing cooperation. The exercises here are divided into those for different-sized groupings. Clearly there can be no cooperation exercises for individuals! Below you can find activities for pairs, small groups and the whole class.

Paired cooperation exercises

Walk with instructions

- *Work in pairs.*
- *One person closes their eyes.*
- *The other must guide their partner around the room.*
- *Use only your voice to give whispered instructions in your partner's ear.*
- *You must not bump into anyone else.*
- *What skills are you using here?*

Obstacle course

- *Set up an 'obstacle course' consisting of chairs, tables, etc.*
- *In pairs, you must guide your partner through the obstacle course.*
- *You can only use your voice, again whispering instructions in the person's ear.*
- *What skills are you using here?*
- *As well as cooperating with a partner, the other person must trust you to guide them correctly.*

No

- *In pairs, name yourselves 'A' and 'B'.*
- *Person 'A' should make a series of suggestions to Person 'B' about what they should do.*
- *Person 'B' should answer 'no' to every suggestion.*

- *Person 'A' – how does this make you feel?*
- *What atmosphere does this create in the classroom as a whole? Why is this?*
- *This is known as 'blocking'. Why would 'blocking' be a problem in an improvisation or a performance?*

Yes, but

- *Now repeat the exercise.*
- *This time, Person 'A' again makes a series of suggestions to Person 'B'.*
- *This time, though, 'B' should say 'Yes, but . . .' each time, giving a reason why they cannot do what 'A' is suggesting.*
- *Person 'A' – how does this make you feel?*
- *Is it better or worse than when 'B' just said 'no' to everything?*
- *Has the atmosphere in the classroom changed?*

Yes, and

- *Repeat the exercise again.*
- *This time, for every suggestion Person 'A' makes, Person 'B' says 'Yes, and then we could . . .'.*
- *What happens to the atmosphere in the classroom during this exercise?*
- *Why does it change?*

Small group cooperation exercises

Letter/number shapes

- *Work in a small group.*
- *Make the letter/number I call out using your bodies.*
- *You only have ten seconds each time to complete the task.*
- *What skill do you have to use?*

Move the chair

- *Work in groups of four to six.*
- *You have a chair.*

41

- *You must get it from one end of the room to the other.*
- *No one is allowed to walk with it. Go!*
- *This is a race – what do you have to do to win?*

Move the chair (2)

- *Work in the same groups.*
- *Again, you have a chair and must get it across the room.*
- *You are allowed to use two other chairs to help you.*
- *This time no one is allowed to touch the floor.*
- *Talk about why the group that won were successful.*
- *Sometimes this exercise works better if one student takes on the role of 'director' and the others do what that person says.*
- *Why is it sometimes better to put one person in charge of an activity?*

On the table

- Work in groups of five to eight, depending on the size of the tables you have (make it difficult to do).
- *You have one table.*
- *It is a life raft and your ship has sunk.*
- *You must get every member of your group onto the raft. Go!*
- Be careful that the students do not get over-excited and risk hurting themselves.
- Use this exercise when the students are already cooperating well with each other.

'I'm falling!'

- Work in a small group.
- One person stands in the middle. The others make a circle around this person.
- Keeping a rigid body shape, the person should shout 'I'm falling!' and then 'fall'.
- The others must catch the person.
- Again, do this when you feel you can trust the students to take it seriously.
- *This is about trust as well as cooperation.*
- *What happens if you don't trust or cooperate with your group?*

Whole-class cooperation exercises

Leader of the band

- A volunteer goes outside.
- The class chooses someone to be the 'leader' of the band.
- The volunteer returns.
- The class performs a series of movements (clapping, tapping knees, patting floor, etc.), following the 'leader'.
- *Try to change movements at exactly the same moment as the leader, so that it's not clear exactly who the leader is.*
- The volunteer must try and guess who the 'leader' is.
- *How are we cooperating here?*
- *What happens if we do not cooperate?*
- *Is there anything that makes it harder or easier for us to cooperate?*

Walk and freeze

- *Stand in a space.*
- *Working as a whole class, walk around the space.*
- *Freeze as a whole class then move off again, without using any signals.*
- *This is similar to the exercise with the drum ('Walk and freeze') but you have no signal to stop.*
- *You have to cooperate as a whole class to do this.*

Use the chair

- *Stand in a circle.*
- Put a chair in the centre.
- The class must 'use' the chair as different objects, for example, a car seat, a lawnmower, a sink, etc.
- If the chair is not in 'use' and the teacher sits on it, the class 'loses'.
- Make it harder by insisting that each student is only allowed one go each and when they have had their turn they must sit down. This forces everyone to get involved.
- *What skills are you having to use here?*

Pass the clap

- Don't be put off by the name of this one, it's great fun!
- Stand the class in a circle.
- *We are going to pass a clap around the circle. The clap starts with me* [the teacher].
- *Turn your body to the left or the right to 'pass' the clap on to the next person.*
- *Once you receive the clap, immediately pass it on again, either to your left or right.*
- *The idea is to create a continuous sound of clapping, with a smooth rhythm and no gaps or missed beats.*
- To get everyone involved, start by passing the clap in a clockwise direction, right the way around the circle.
- Next, pass it all the way back anticlockwise.
- Now, allow the students to pass it either to the left or right.
- Once they have got the hang of this, pass two (or even more) claps simultaneously.
- *What do we all have to do* [i.e. cooperate, focus] *to make this work?*

Confidence

By its very nature as a performance art, drama does require a degree of confidence. Funnily enough, it does not necessarily follow that your most confident students are going to be 'best' at the subject. Highly confident children are typically very good at the performance-based activities, but sometimes have trouble in group situations, where they need to defer to other people's ideas.

Even those students in the class who have a total lack of confidence will still be able to gain a great deal from drama lessons, particularly from the exercises that are not based around performing. And of course, the more drama the children do, the more confident they will become.

There are a few general rules that it is wise to follow when you are trying to encourage your shy children to become more confident.

- Accept that some children will adopt a fairly passive role in lessons, taking part but essentially opting out by the way they approach the tasks.
- Don't push shy students before they're ready, or put them on the spot.
- When working with the whole class together, for instance in a circle, it's wise to allow individuals to 'pass' if they wish.
- Think about how your quieter children can participate, particularly in performances. For instance, they might take on the role of director or costume designer.
- Where a student does completely opt out, sitting to one side and refusing to take part, it can work best to simply ignore the child. Often, when they see how much fun the rest of the class is having, they decide to join in.

Confidence-boosting exercises

You can find some exercises below designed to develop your students' confidence. While confidence may take time to develop for some children, when it does it will be a great benefit for them in a range of other school subjects.

Individual confidence exercises

Shy walking

- *Stand in a space on your own.*
- *Imagine you are very shy.*
- *Now begin to walk around the room as though you are very shy.*
- *What kind of body language and facial expressions do you use?*
- *How do you interact with others when you pass them?*

Confident walking

- *Now repeat the exercise, this time as though you are very confident.*
- *What kind of body language and facial expressions do you use now?*

- *How do you interact with others when you pass them?*
- *Make the contrast between the two very sharp.*

Paired confidence exercises

Shy talking

- *Stand in a space with a partner.*
- *Imagine you are very shy.*
- *Count between yourselves from one to 20, with the first person saying one to five, the second six to ten, and so on. Speak as though you are very timid.*
- *What kind of voice did you use? Did your shyness have an impact on your facial expressions?*
- *What was the overall atmosphere during the exercise?*

Confident talking

- *Now repeat the exercise, this time as though you are both very confident.*
- *What kind of voice and facial expressions did you use?*
- *Again, what kind of atmosphere did you create with your partner?*

Whole-class confidence exercises

Say something good

- The whole class stands in a circle.
- Everyone should think of one good thing to say about the person to their left.
- Go around the circle, with each student stepping forward to say something good about this person.

Strike a pose

- Stand the class in a circle.
- Going around the circle, the first student steps forward, strikes a pose, then steps back.
- The rest of the students step in, strike the same pose then step back.

46

- Repeat going all the way around the circle, with each student taking a turn.

'Overcoming shyness'

- Set up a chat show in the style of Oprah Winfrey's, Trisha's, etc.
- Ask for volunteers to play the host, panel of experts and guests.
- The other students act as the audience.
- Improvise a show about 'overcoming shyness'.
- Guests come on the show to talk about how they were shy and how they overcame it.
- If your students are not yet experienced at doing whole-class improvisations, take on the role of the host so that you can control the drama from within.

4

Warm-ups and cool-downs

In this chapter, I give some thoughts about why warming up and cooling down is a good idea. You'll find lots of ideas for short exercises and games that you can use to warm up your children at the beginning of a drama period. You'll also find suggestions for 'cool downs' – ways of finishing off a session that will help the students calm themselves down and get physically and mentally ready for the next lesson.

Why warm up?

There are plenty of very good reasons for doing a warm-up at the start of a drama session. Just as children will warm up their bodies for PE, so they should be shown the importance of doing the same for drama.

- Drama is a physical activity – doing warm-ups will help your children get their bodies and voices ready to be used.
- Doing a warm-up will help avoid the injuries that might happen to a 'cold' voice or body.
- Your students will often have come from an academic lesson in which they were sitting at desks. Getting their bodies moving and their voices working will help you get them in the mood for drama.

- Warm-up exercises make a great starter activity – they are short, fun and focused.
- With everyone doing a warm-up together, this helps develop the feeling that the whole class is a unit. This is often an essential element for a successful lesson.

Physical warm-ups

Ways of walking

Getting the class moving around the space is a great way of warming up your students at the start of a drama lesson. It's not as simple as it might sound, though! At first you will probably find that the children end up walking in a large circle. You will need to encourage them to:

- use all the available space
- move in lots of different directions rather than in a circle
- be aware of where other students are in the room
- avoid physical contact with people, furniture or walls
- have a sense of focus – feel that they are *going* somewhere.

From this starting point, you can bring in loads of different ways of walking around the room. You can find plenty of suggestions below. You'll also find some similar walking exercises in the section on concentration (see p. 35–7). Once you get the hang of how these activities work, you'll be able to think up lots more ideas of your own.

Walk and turn

- *Walk, with focus, in one direction. Go* towards *something (e.g. a wall).*
- *When you get to where you are going, immediately turn and walk* towards *something else (e.g. a window).*

Walk with hazards
Move around the room as though you are walking . . .

- *through an icy wilderness.*
- *during a stormy night.*
- *up a muddy hillside.*
- *across a pile of nails.*

Walk in a mood
Walk around the room as though you are feeling . . .

- *terrified.*
- *happy.*
- *furious.*
- *ecstatic.*
- *depressed.*
- *paranoid.*
- *serene.*

Walk as a character
Move around the room as though you are a . . .

- *police officer.*
- *monster.*
- *king or queen.*
- *sumo wrestler.*

Walk my walk
This can be done in a couple of different ways, as described below.

- A volunteer shows his or her normal walk to the class.
- The rest of the students copy the walk as closely as they can.
  OR
- A volunteer demonstrates a 'funny walk' to the class.
- The other students all join in, doing the funny walk as well.

Shoal of fish

- A 'leader' fish is selected.
- The whole class follows the leader fish.

- When the leader changes direction, the whole shoal goes with him or her.

Ways of moving

As well as walking around the space in different ways, there are also lots of other physical warm-ups that you can use. You'll find plenty of suggestions below. These activities are great for developing your students' cooperation and concentration skills, and they are also a lot of fun. Hopefully, they should help get your children enthused and ready to do some drama.

Surfer dudes

- *Stand in a space on your own.*
- *Position yourself in a semi-crouch, i.e. knees half bent, body upright.*
- *Imagine you are on a surfboard.*
- *Go surfing!*
- To add to the fun, the teacher might give a commentary about the size of the waves.

Puppets

- Work in pairs: one student is the puppet, the other the puppet master.
- The puppet has [imaginary] strings all over his or her body.
- Depending on the age of the children, these can be on the hands, elbows, shoulders, feet, knees, head, and even on each of the fingers.
- The puppet master must move his or her puppet around, using only the strings.
- The puppet must focus carefully to ensure that the imaginary strings appear to be real.
- Once they get the hang of it, encourage your students to move their puppets around the room.
- The puppets can then interact with each other, for instance by shaking hands.

Mould clay

- Work in pairs: one student is the lump of clay, the other the sculptor.
- The sculptor must sculpt and position his or her clay into an interesting pose.
- When they have all finished, the sculptors can take a walk around the room to look at other people's models.
- Swap the pairs over, so that the roles are reversed.

Master/servant

- This fun activity is a variation of 'Simon Says . . .'. It can be done in pairs or as a whole class.
- In pairs, one person is the 'master', the other the 'servant'.
- The servant must do everything the master says, e.g. 'stand up', 'sit down', 'spin around', etc.
- The master must not ask the student to do anything dangerous or demeaning.
- After a couple of minutes, stop the class and swap the students over.
- To do this activity with the whole class, chose one student to be the master (I tend to use the chance to be master as a reward – it's very popular!). The rest of the students are the servants, and must do everything their master says. If you're willing, it's a great idea for the teacher to join in as a servant as well.

Tug-of-war

- Split the class into groups of about eight students, then pair each group up with another.
- The two groups each create a line, one opposite each other, like the two teams in a tug-of-war.
- They hold an imaginary rope.
- On your signal, the tug-of-war begins!

Vocal warm-ups

We sometimes assume that our children don't need too much in the way of vocal warm-ups. I wonder if this comes from experiencing their normal level of chatter during the typical school day. Where a drama session is going to be particularly voice intensive, or when the students are going to be performing in a large space where they must project their voices, it is a good idea to do a vocal warm-up as well as a physical one.

Word tennis

- There are various ways to do this exercise – why not experiment to find some more approaches of your own?
- The students work in pairs, standing opposite a partner.
- Give a topic, for instance 'the weather'.
- When you say 'go', the students freely discuss this topic.
- They say one word each, back and forth, like a game of tennis.
- This can also be done with a tighter focus.
  - o For instance, each word must start with the last letter of the previous one (i.e. using the topic of animals, the students might say 'elephant', 'tiger', 'rhinoceros', and so on).

Nonsense insults

- Work with a partner.
- The first person hurls a nonsense insult at the other, for instance 'You're a purple-gilled pinkyponky ming moo!'
- The other person then replies with another nonsense insult, and so forth.

Be my friend? (1)

- Working in pairs, make friends with your partner.
- Now get into an argument.
- Storm off and start again with another person.

Be my friend? (2)

- Repeat the above exercise, but this time use numbers rather than words.
- For instance, the first person says '1, 2, 3', the second replies '4, 5' and so on.
- Again, make friends, then fall out, then move on to another person.

Sausages

- Again working in pairs, one person asks a series of questions.
- The other person answers 'sausage' to every question.
- The aim is to go for as long as you can without laughing.

Why cool down?

Drama is not an isolated event in the school day. Your students will always be doing something afterwards, whether this is moving on to another teacher in the secondary school, into another lesson with you in the primary school, or heading home if it's the end of the day.

As an English teacher, I have witnessed the effects on my students when they have come from an active or very exciting lesson. It can take me a substantial part of my teaching time to calm them down and get them into the mood to focus on written work. A great deal of adrenalin can be produced in your students during the course of a drama lesson. This is especially so when they have done a performance or some particularly exciting work.

To calm them down, you might try some of the following exercises. I've made a habit of incorporating some of these into pretty much every lesson I teach (in drama and also in other subjects). It really helps me to calm down the class so that the students leave in a composed frame of mind.

Cool-down exercises

Statues

- Get yourselves into a comfortable position. You could sit on the floor, or lay down if you prefer. (This can also be done at desks – in a classroom you could suggest that the students lay their heads on their arms.)
- When I say 'go', you must freeze like a statue. You must not move, blink, fidget – the only thing you are allowed to do is breathe (they do tend to ask).
- You must freeze completely still for a set length of time (two minutes is about right to start with). As the students become more adept at this, encourage them to freeze for longer and longer periods of time.
- You might use the time to give some praise for work done in the lesson, to give ideas for improvements in certain areas, a reminder about homework, or simply to relax yourself.

Stretch and flop

- Stand by yourself in a space.
- Stretch your arms above your head as high as you can, rising onto your tiptoes.
- As you do this, imagine you are a puppet being stretched up by the person holding your strings.
- Now imagine that the strings are cut.
- Drop your arms down first, then your head, then your shoulders and your body, until you are bent over at the waist. Keep your knees slightly bent so that you don't pull any muscles.
- Very slowly, bend your knees even further and sink to the floor so that you end up in a heap.

Close observation

- Working on your own, choose a prop and take it to a space.
- Sit down and spend a few minutes looking at it in great detail.
- Do this in complete silence.

- At the end of the time talk about what your students have observed.

Meditation

- Sit or lie down in a space on your own, away from any distractions.
- Close your eyes and imagine a clear blue sky.
- You are going to try to empty your mind of all thoughts.
- When a thought does intrude, try to see it as a cloud and allow it to slowly float away.
- It is harder than you might think to completely clear your mind – monks spend many years learning how to meditate effectively.

Slow the rhythm

- Sit in a space on your own.
- We are going to clap a rhythm together, starting fast and gradually slowing down until we stop.
- The teacher starts – choose a fairly simple rhythm, for instance two long claps and three short ones.
- Start using quite a fast speed.
- Wait until everyone has joined in and the whole class is clapping together.
- Now very gradually slow the speed down.
- Aim for everyone to stop clapping at exactly the same moment.

What did you learn today?

- Sit in a space with your eyes closed.
- Think of one activity or exercise that you did in today's lesson.
- Remember all the good things that you or your group did during that exercise. How could you bring these positive attributes into play next time around?
- Now remember any areas where you or your group might have made improvements. Think about how you could make these changes in our next drama session.

5

Aspects of drama

In this chapter, you'll find information and ideas about the different aspects of drama – that is, the elements that go together to create a piece of theatre. For each of the different aspects of drama given here, I offer advice, ideas and activities for using these in a drama lesson. You might like to devise a scheme of work in which each of these aspects are covered in turn, or you could simply incorporate some of the exercises into a one-off drama session.

Inspiration

Any piece of art, whether a painting, a novel, a play, or a song, will have an inspiration of some kind. Inspiration provides the initial 'spark' for the act of creation. Inspiration can come from pretty much any source. Sometimes, the teacher will provide an inspirational idea or resource; sometimes, the students will find their own source of inspiration. When you're looking for ideas, consider what offers really interesting dramatic possibilities. If you get really stuck, I always find that if I look around myself wherever I am I can see a few items or images that I might use for inspiration. For instance, right now I can see an empty cardboard box that could prove really inspirational.

Here are some suggestions to get you started:

- music – both classical and modern

- sound effects
- news stories and headlines
- news headlines – in newspapers and on television
- props – any interesting objects
- costumes, hats, shoes, bags
- sayings, quotes, snippets of dialogue
- lighting effects – blackout, torches, green lighting gels
- a setting – on the moon, in a haunted castle
- a picture or a photo
- an item from nature, such as a leaf or a stone
- an interesting person
- a character from a story.

Using inspiration

- Show the class three dramatic headlines.
- Discuss how these might inspire a piece of drama.
- Split the students into small groups. Ask them to produce a frozen picture to summarize each headline.
- Show the freezes to the class.
- The students must guess which headline is being portrayed.
- Now ask the students to develop a planned improvisation using the headline as inspiration.
- This should be a news report with a news person in the studio telling the story, and a reporter interviewing witnesses or those involved at the scene.

Storytelling

The story is a great starting point for drama – of course the vast majority of plays involve the telling of a story. Your children are likely to be very familiar with stories, and comfortable with using them. You will find traditional stories, such as nursery rhymes, fairy tales and myths, particularly useful, as all or most of your students will know them. Of course it is also great to use stories from a variety of cultures and from a diverse range of traditions.

It is useful to spend some time discussing how stories work, how they might feed into drama, and how we can use them most effectively to create a piece of theatre. For instance, you might ask:

- *What stories do you know already?*
- *How do we get inspiration for a story?*
- *What makes a good story?*
- *What is structure and why do we need it?*
- *How can we tell where the beginning, middle and end of a story come?*
- *How do we show when we've reached the end of the story?* (You might well find that you need to overcome the problem of the children finishing their play and saying 'that's it', rather than understanding how to bring it to a clear and satisfying end.)

Actor/storyteller

- This is a fun warm-up activity.
- *Work in pairs – one person is the actor, the other is the storyteller.*
- *The storyteller tells the story; the actor acts it out as they speak.*
- *The story might be mundane (what I did this morning) or exciting (the bank raid).*
- This exercise can also be done as a whole class, with you or a confident student taking on the part of the storyteller.

Subverting tradition

- It can be great fun to take a traditional story and subvert the audience's expectations.
- For instance, improvising a documentary based around the story of the Three Little Pigs, but from the wolf's perspective.
- The documentary might be called 'The Wolf's Story: Wolfie bites back!'
- Similarly, you might retell a nursery rhyme ('Humpty Dumpty') using a different form, for instance as an opera or a rap.

Tag story

- The whole class sits in a circle.
- Two students start an improvisation (on any subject) in the centre.
- After a while, the teacher 'freezes' them.
- A volunteer enters and takes up the frozen position of one of the actors.
- When the teacher says 'go', this new person restarts the improvisation, but must change the subject.
- The 'new' subject should take its inspiration from the frozen position, but could be a completely different story.
- This really is instant improvisation – there is no time to plan what will happen.
- The other person will have to work out the scenario from what you do and say.

Props

A prop (or, more correctly, a property) is anything that is brought onto the stage during the course of a performance. Pretty much anything you like can be used as a prop, and this means that props are a great way for the teacher with few resources to 'spice up' his or her drama lessons.

From where I'm writing this, I can see hundreds of props that I might take into a classroom to inspire some drama. For instance: a peg, a book, a ruler, a mug, a globe, an empty cardboard box, even a radiator key.

Magic props

- Work as a whole class, standing in a circle.
- Say: *I have some magic invisible props to show you.*
- Produce each invisible item (perhaps from a bag or box), passing it around the circle.
- You might like to either:
  - show what the item is by the way that you interact with it first

  o allow the students to show what it is by the way they pass it around.

Props auction

- Work as a whole class, standing in a circle.
- Show the class a simple prop, for instance a peg.
- Now ask for volunteers to auction the prop to the rest of the class.
- The students must 'talk up' the prop so that everyone wants to buy it.

Ring ring

- Put a phone in the middle of the circle.
- When it rings, a volunteer must enter the circle and answer it.
- A short improvisation takes place.
- When the phone call ends, the volunteer returns to the circle.
- The phone rings again . . .

Costume

Depending on your situation, you might have a range of costumes with which to work and teach. Alternatively, it might be a case of scrabbling around to see what you can find at home. It is definitely worth asking for contributions to a 'costume cupboard' if you feel inspired to create one and you have a suitable space available. Here are a few words of advice.

- Be selective – don't include just any old clothes that you are given. Before you know it, your costume cupboard will look like a jumble sale.
- Consider the size of your children. If you're working in Key Stage One, most adult clothes will be way too big for them. With younger children, accessories such as hats, shoes, bags, etc. will probably be more useful.
- Have some way of sorting the clothes – for instance, having labelled boxes for smaller items such as scarves and hats.

- A rail of some kind is indispensable for keeping the clothes relatively tidy and easy to access. If you don't have a cupboard available, consider buying a portable clothes rail that you can store in one corner of a room.
- Be ruthless about keeping your costumes tidy, perhaps getting a team of student volunteers to take responsibility for this job.
- Tidy the costumes regularly, perhaps once every term. Always have a tidy up after a school production: in the excitement and chaos of doing the show, the cupboard can easily get trashed.
- Limit access to the cupboard or it is likely to become a free-for-all. A padlock is a worthwhile investment if there isn't a lock on your cupboard.
- Where you only have one item available to use (e.g. one helmet – see below), show it to the class as an inspiration, but ask them to improvise using an imaginary version.
- When and if students perform their pieces to the class, offer the chance to use the real thing.

'Naughty' clothes

Working individually, the students improvise various items of clothing that seem to have a life of their own. For instance, the:

- helmet that won't fasten
- gloves that won't go on
- shoes that refuse to walk
- hat that keeps falling off.

Ways of wearing a scarf

- Working either individually or in pairs, the students experiment with different kinds of scarf, and different ways of wearing them.
- Each type of scarf/way of wearing it could lead on to a different kind of character.
- For instance, a chiffon scarf slung nonchalantly over the shoulder might suggest a snobbish lady.

The bus queue

- Show the class a variety of hats, e.g. a bike helmet, a builder's hat, a bowler hat and an old lady's woolly bobble hat.
- Ask a small group of volunteers to each take a hat.
- Get them to improvise a scene at a bus stop, each one entering in turn.
- The characters that they chose should be based around the hats they are wearing.

The mystery bag

- Fill an interesting bag or suitcase with some props.
- Explain that the bag was left behind somewhere (a crime scene, an airport luggage carousel, in the staffroom).
- The students must decide on what kind of person owns this bag, based on what is inside.
- They could use this character as a starting point for an improvisation.
- You might choose a really wacky set of contents for your bag. For instance, one teacher told me she filled a suitcase with bananas and that this stimulated some really interesting stories.

Setting – place and time

In the theatre, a stage set will be used to create a setting for a play. The set designer will create a set that he or she feels suits the geographical and historical setting of the play. The set design will often echo the storyline of the play in some way as well. As well as the stage set, there are other elements that go together to create the setting, and these include lighting, sound effects, music, costume, etc.

Although you obviously can't recreate a full stage set in your classroom, there are lots of really fascinating activities that you can do to give an idea of setting.

Individual focus

- *Sit in a space on your own.*
- *Close your eyes and breathe deeply for a few moments.*
- *Now picture a time and place, using your senses as fully as you can.*
- *For example, picture a prehistoric desert landscape. See the kind of clothes that the people wore, feel the heat of the sun, hear the animals prowling around, smell the meat as it cooks on the fire.*
- *Now try a New York street on a Saturday night at midnight. The nightclubs are just emptying out, all around you are city sounds, such as traffic, taxis, police sirens. See the reflections on the wet streets, hear the singing of the drunks and snatches of music escaping from the clubs.*
- Talk afterwards about the kind of things the children saw, heard, etc.

Whole-class focus

- Sit the whole class in a circle.
- Give a setting (place and time) to the class.
- The students give a stream of images, taking turns, going around the circle.
- For instance, an emergency room in hospital on a Friday night; the school playground in the build up to a fight.

Small-group improvisations

- Divide your room up by marking off squares with four chairs.
- Split the class up into small groups (about four to six students in each one).
- Each group has one square of space, indicated by the four chairs.
- Now give a series of settings as before, incorporating a sense of time, place and occasion wherever possible.
- When you say 'go', the group must immediately go into an improvisation in that setting.
- There should be no discussion. The students will need to be

very alert to what the others in their group are doing, and also willing to adapt their own ideas to fit what happens.

- When you say 'freeze', they stop and you give the next setting. Here are some ideas:

  o celebrations at the end of the Second World War, on a street in London
  o a moment after the assassination of President Kennedy
  o ten seconds after England won the 1966 football World Cup final
  o ten seconds after England lost to Germany in the 1990 World Cup semi-final
  o Trafalgar Square, midnight, New Year's Eve, 1999
  o five minutes after a lift broke down.

Creating atmosphere

A key part of the magic of theatre is that wonderful thing known as atmosphere. There really is nothing quite like the excitement of a live performance – so, whenever you get the chance, do take your students on trips to the theatre. It really is worth the time and effort involved to show them just how magical drama can be.

Creating an atmosphere in drama sessions is a great way of getting your students engaged with the subject. For those lucky teachers who have lights, using different coloured gels can make a huge difference to the 'feel' of the room. However, there are plenty of options available to all teachers, even if you don't have a dedicated drama space or good equipment. You could try the following.

- Play music that fits the 'mood' of the topic you're covering.
- Use sound effects: buy these on CD, or download them from the internet. You can also get your students to make them (see 'Circle sound effects', p. 66).
- Play different instruments at different speeds. For example, discuss the difference in atmosphere created by a slow, rhythmic drum beat and a fast, erratic one.

- Try out lighting effects such as coloured lights, blackouts, fairy lights and torches.
- Use costumes and pieces of material. For instance, something sinister or dangerous hidden under a sheet could make a good starting point for an improvisation.
- Focus on colours – choosing costumes, props and lights around a single colour can make a symbolic statement, for instance all red creates a dramatic effect that suggests danger, all green lights makes for a rather spooky atmosphere.

Walking with hazards

- Repeat the 'walk with hazards' exercise from Chapter 4 (p. 49–50).
- This time, add in some sound effects such as squelching through mud or the howling wind of the storm.

The alley

- Get the class to create a 'conscience alley', as explained on p. 26.
- Ask for a volunteer to go down the alley.
- Choose a scenario filled with atmosphere. For instance, walking through a haunted wood at midnight on Halloween.
- As the person passes, the other students create atmosphere by adding sound effects and voices.

Circle sound effects

- Get the whole class to lay down in a circle, heads to the centre, feet outwards.
- Their ears should be almost touching for the best effect.
- Now give a setting (see 'Setting – place and time' above for lots of ideas – p. 63–5).
- The students must create the sound effects and voices that might be heard in that setting. For example, in a:
  o Victorian asylum
  o rainforest
  o football match

- o zoo
- o machine.
- Not everyone needs to be making a noise at once.
- You will find that the students soon get the hang of it.
- When they are comfortable with this, ask them to create a 'sound track'.
- To do this, they must start quietly, gradually build up to a crescendo, then either stop abruptly or fade back out again.
- It is possible to do this without anyone giving a signal, so long as they all listen carefully to each other.
- You might like to tape some of their efforts, so that they can listen to them afterwards and perhaps even use them in a performance.

Haunted house

- *It's Halloween, and a group of children dare each other to enter a haunted house.*
- Choose three or four volunteers to be the children. Give them a couple of torches to use during their improvisation.
- Split the rest of the class into small groups and ask each group to create some spooky furniture for each room of the house. For instance, paintings with eyes that move, a clock which grabs anyone who walks past.
- Talk with the class about what will make their acting genuinely scary.
- Get the whole class into position, with each group providing one room of the house.
- If possible, darken the room to create more atmosphere.
- Begin the improvisation. The children arrive at the house and talk about how scared they are. They enter and the story develops, as they look around the rooms.
- Allow your actors to create their own story: they might get split up, one might be hurt or trapped, etc. Encourage the children to talk as they move through the house, creating a narration that builds the story.

Contrasts

Contrasts offer a good way of adding interest, tension and excitement to a piece of drama. Many of the best stories are about a contrast of some kind – between rich and poor, young and old, love and hate. Shakespeare was a great fan of contrasts and opposites; many of his plays are full of opposing forces. These forces provide the themes that run through plays such as *Romeo and Juliet* – love and hate, young and old, night and day.

From one to the other (1)

- *Stand in a space on your own.*
- *As you hear the opposites, move from one to the other on the spot. Aim to move gradually between the two ends of the spectrum.*
- *Take about half a minute to change from one to the other.* You might like to play some music while the students do this activity.
- Here are some ideas for contrasts to use:
  o down to up
  o small to big
  o silent to noisy
  o cold to hot
  o young to old.
- *When you've completed the journey in one direction, go backwards, so that you go from old to young, up to down, etc.*

From one to the other (2)

- *Stand in a space on your own.*
- *For each pair of contrasts, take ten steps to move from one to the other.*
- The students could brainstorm the words for these.
- *Each step should give a gradual change, e.g. tiny, small, little, medium, etc. and so on, through to enormous.*
- You might like to use ten drumbeats to help the students all do this at the same time.
- Again, once the journey has been done in one direction, you could get the students to take ten steps backwards to reverse it.

Yes and no

- *Yes and no are a fascinating pair of contrasts. At their simplest, they can mean the complete opposite. But . . .*
- *With a partner, try different nuances of saying 'yes' and 'no'.*
- *For instance, a 'yes' that is very hesitant and actually means 'I'm not quite sure'. Or a 'no' that is more like a shocked exclamation.*
- *See how many different kinds of 'yes' and 'no' you can find.*
- *Can you say 'yes' and actually mean 'no', and vice versa?*

Selecting material

Your students will need to learn how to select and use appropriate material, particularly when they are developing an idea for performance. The inclination at first can be to include every aspect of what happens in a particular scenario. Of course, plays do often tell a story, but not every detail is included or the play would be either rather dull or very, very long.

Talk with your class about what might make interesting material for a performance, with plenty of dramatic potential and engagement for the audience. For instance:

- an idea with opposing themes, so that the audience feels pulled in two directions
- a scenario with lots of dramatic tension, where 'what happens next?' becomes the driving force for both actors and audience
- a scenario with a surprise in it where, just as the audience is getting comfortable, something shocking happens
- a story with really fascinating characters – people who are vibrant, odd, crazy, bold, brave, or people who the audience will associate closely with.

The heart of the story

- Work as a whole class, sitting in a circle.
- Get the students to retell some familiar stories, for instance a fairytale such as *Cinderella* or a fable such as *The Hare and the Tortoise*.

69

- You might read out a fairly long version of the story, or perhaps ask the children to tell the story going round the circle, one section or sentence at a time.
- If your class tend to get restless, you might also have some students acting out the story as it is told, as in the exercise actor/storyteller (see p. 59).
- Split the class into pairs or small groups.
- Ask them to retell the story, but with a narrow focus, so that they are forced to select the really important material. You might ask them to do one of the following:
  - produce three freeze-frames to tell the whole story
  - tell the story using exactly 20 words
  - devise a news bulletin that tells the whole story in only 30 seconds.
- Watch the groups perform. Afterwards, discuss how and why certain parts of the stories were selected.

Themes

A theme provides you with an underlying thread or idea, which you can link the learning to over several lessons. Pretty much anything could be used as a theme; for some of my ideas, see Chapter 9. Here are some other suggestions as to what you could use:

- a curriculum focus taken from and linked with another subject, for instance 'Forces' in science
- an abstract concept or idea, such as 'Love' or 'Division'
- a theme inspired by a character or book, or developed from a playscript, for example *Across the Barricades* by Joan Lingard
- an idea linked to a media form such as television, for instance 'The 'Estate' theme covered in Chapter 9 (which has obvious links to soap operas)
- a PSHE-related issue, such as 'Bullying' or 'Teenage Pregnancy'
- an idea that relates closely to character, for example 'Young and Old' or 'Runaway'
- a genre-based theme, such as 'Crime' or 'Ghosts'

- a theme that looks closely at a drama skill or technique, for instance 'Dramatic Tension'.

Inevitably, some themes work better than others in creating good material for drama. When choosing a theme, there are certain elements to look out for:

- something with human interest or a moral question at its heart
- an idea that the students will relate closely to their lives outside school
- a theme with plenty of opportunities for creating dramatic tension
- an idea for which you have a lot of related props, costumes, etc.
- a theme that links into some cross-curricular work, with some interesting characters that the children might play
- something that asks the students to think deeply and to widen their understanding of other people's viewpoints
- an approach that develops the students' drama skills and helps them understand certain techniques more fully.

When planning for a theme, there are various approaches that you might take, often depending on the kind of theme you have chosen. You might do one of these.

- Take a chronological look at a subject, as in the approach used for the theme of 'War' in Chapter 9 (p. 147–59).
- Look at different aspects of the theme in turn, for instance studying how dramatic tension can be created by body language one week, confined spaces the next, and so on.
- Use a range of locations in which the theme might be featured. For example, bullying at school, at work, in the home.
- Look at the theme from a range of character perspectives. So, with 'Crime', you might be police detectives one week, then criminals, lawyers and judges, victims, etc. after that.

You can find ideas for both primary and secondary drama towards the end of the book, in Chapter 9. This chapter gives lesson-by-lesson suggestions for approaching and working with four different themes.

Forms

The form or format of a piece of drama simply means the structure within which it is presented. Formats can come from a range of media – television, literature, music, and so on. Offering the children an interesting format within which to work can be enough to inspire some really great drama. The form that is used will have an effect on the overall presentation. For instance, on:

- the characters that are featured
- the language and dialogue used
- the length and structure of the performance
- whether it is serious, funny, informative, etc.
- what sort of props, costumes, and furniture is featured
- the locations and settings that are used.

Because different forms have typical, traditional features, a good way of making any format even more engaging is to play around with the audience's expectations. For instance, the audience expects an opera to be rather highbrow and performed by mature, well-spoken singers. An opera set on a London estate, featuring kids who sing in slang, would confound what the audience usually expects to see. (See also 'Subverting tradition' in the section on storytelling on p. 59).

Here are lots of ideas for formats that could be used either in a straightforward way or with some kind of twist:

- interview
- TV news report
- newspaper story
- chat show
- documentary
- opera
- reality programme

- fairytale
- fable
- match report
- musical
- children's story
- soap opera
- advert
- rap
- pop song
- children's TV programme.

Genre

Genre is a French word, literally meaning 'type'. In the context of drama, a genre is a particular type of story, for instance crime, horror or romance. There are some very good reasons why you might use genre as a starting point.

- It's a great way of inspiring your children to produce good quality drama.
- Many genres (action, supernatural, horror, etc.) are naturally full of dramatic tension, and consequently using them encourages your students to build suspense into their performances.
- Similarly, many genres come with a built-in sense of atmosphere, and again this will help your students to develop this facet of their work.
- The students will be very familiar with certain genres from watching television and films. Crime (*CSI, The Bill*) and medicine (*House, Holby City*) are particularly popular genres at the moment.

Each genre has a set of typical features that your students can use to help them create a piece of drama. For instance, the:

- storyline
- setting
- places

- characters
- events
- props
- costumes
- atmosphere.

To give an example, in the action genre, you might have:

- a storyline – an evil villain is trying to destroy the world, only the hero can stop him
- a setting – an exotic island with a secret underwater entrance
- places – a casino, an aeroplane, a helicopter or fast car
- characters – a hunky hero, a beautiful heroine, an evil villain
- events – our hero has only 24 hours to save the world from the villain's evil plan
- props – guns, gadgets, ropes
- costumes – black jumpsuits, balaclavas, black suit and tie
- atmosphere – fast-moving, exciting.

Here are some suggestions for exercises to use in various different genres. In the secondary setting, you might like to explore one genre a week over the course of a half-term. In a primary school, the genre theme can tie in nicely with a range of different literacy and topic work.

Horror

- The story is based in a deserted, shut-down museum of horror.
- The students will play animatronic exhibits that come to life.
- Brainstorm with the whole class to gather ideas for potential exhibits, for instance, *Frankenstein, Dracula,* etc.
- Split the class into small groups. The students must create a short 'scene'. When the button on the exhibit is pressed, the characters come to life, perform the scene, then the exhibit shuts down again.
- Give the groups time to prepare their exhibits.
- Cover each exhibit with a white sheet.
- Get a couple of volunteers to play two children who have

broken into the museum of horror at night.
- The children have torches. They search around the museum, talking about what they are doing and how they are feeling.
- When they lift each sheet, they press the button to make each exhibit come to life.
- Once they have looked at each exhibit, something begins to go wrong.
- The exhibits come to life and begin to move towards the children.

Science fiction

- Set up the classroom as a space ship.
- The ship has been deserted for some reason (the students can decide on the reason or let it develop during the improvisation).
- There are bodies lying everywhere, some still alive, others dead from something horrible.
- The furniture and equipment is in disarray.
- Three volunteers beam onto the ship holding torches. As they explore, they build a narrative together.
- You can also do this exercise with an alien loose on board – the children love to play the alien, so choose a volunteer who really deserves it.

War
There's a whole scheme based around the subject of war further on in the book (see p. 147–59). Many of the ideas in that scheme could be adapted to use with students of different ages.

Soap opera
As a genre, soap opera seems to be very popular with students. It offers a slice of 'real life' in a range of settings. Just like many adults, your students may be avid watchers of particular soaps. The soap opera genre is particularly useful for developing characterization skills, because they typically include a wide range of clearly defined people. When using the genre, you might do one of these.

- Brainstorm a list of soap operas that your students watch, or that they know.
- Brainstorm the kind of settings that are used for soap operas. Discuss how, while these might vary, the majority of action will be set in a fairly small neighbourhood.
- Brainstorm the kind of characters found in soap operas. Aim to identify key types and the features usually connected to these people.
- Ask your students to devise their own soap opera, based on their knowledge of the main features. This could be done as a brief activity; or alternatively as a much longer exercise, to include theme music, a series of scenes, etc.

Comedy

Comedy is a surprisingly tricky genre to teach. You will probably have your 'class clown', who finds it easy to make others laugh. Those students who are not naturally funny can find comedy hard to understand. Children can be cruel, and are fast to laugh at each other's mistakes. I always insist that they do not laugh at a performance unless it is intentionally funny. Being laughed at when you are trying to give a serious performance is potentially very damaging to your students' self-confidence.

It's worth considering the following points before you begin teaching the comedy genre to a class

- Children often think it should be 'easy' to be funny, and will laugh at their own antics during a performance.
- This laughter is typically of the 'covering embarrassment' kind – by laughing they undermine and downplay their own performance before anyone else can. The laughter says, 'See, it wasn't really meant to be serious.'
- When they look at the comedy genre in more detail, students are often surprised by how difficult it is to make an audience laugh.
- Before beginning work on comedy, it's worth talking about the importance of focus. The actors need to be completely deadpan to make the comedy effective.

- You might like to look at some clips from TV and film. Children often respond really well to the slapstick style of Rowan Atkinson in Mr Bean, and to Laurel and Hardy.

Here are some exercises that will help your children practice keeping a straight face.

Poor pussy

- The class stands in a circle.
- One volunteer plays 'pussy'.
- The pussy goes up to students at random, as though it wants a stroke.
- The person selected must say 'poor pussy' and give the pussy a stroke.
- The aim for the pussy is to make the person laugh; the aim for the person stroking is to keep a straight face.

Twister

- This is a good physical warm-up.
- Again, the aim is to keep a straight face at all times.
- Work in pairs. Call out two body parts (*elbow, knee*). The students must join up these two parts of their bodies.
- Once everyone is twisted in position, call out another two parts (*nose, shoulder*).
- The students must keep the first two parts connected, while also joining the next two.
- Keep going until everyone falls over or until they all crack up laughing.

Behind the news

- Two volunteers perform a short improvisation to the class.
- A reporter is 'on the scene' at a really serious news story (a big fire, an armed robbery).
- He or she delivers a report to camera while the class watches.

- The second volunteer is a member of the public.
- He or she makes faces and gestures behind the reporter, making the rest of the class laugh. The reporter must keep a completely straight face the whole time.

Naughty hands

- This one's a classic and the students find it great fun.
- *Get into pairs – for this one it's best to work with a friend. Stand together, one person directly behind the other, facing the same way.*
- *The person in front stands with hands clasped behind his or her back. The person behind puts his or her hands through the crook of the elbows.*
- *These are now the 'naughty hands' that refuse to do as their owner wishes.*
- There are many different scenarios you can use. One of my favourites is a chef – if you add real ingredients this can produce some hilarious, if messy, results. It might be best to spread a plastic mat out first.
- The 'naughty hands' might also:
  o perform an operation
  o cut someone's hair
  o do a painting
  o conduct an orchestra.

Lost in translation

- Work in small groups (this can also be done as a whole-class improvisation when it is performed).
- In the groups, you need a chat show host, a foreign guest or guests, and a translator.
- Set up a row of chairs. The foreign guest has been invited onto the show as an 'expert' on a topic of your choice. Choose something weird or outrageous, with potential for humour, such as 'the mating habits of the Bolivian tree sloth'.
- Play it straight for maximum effect, with plenty of physical humour from the guest. The comedy comes from the deadpan

serious expressions, combined with the outrageous topic and explanation.

- Humour also comes from the difference between the expert's explanation and gestures, and what the translator says.
- For instance, the host asks the foreign guest whether he is enjoying his stay, the guest launches into a tirade which sounds like a series of angry outbursts, they turn to the translator who says (deadpan), 'yes'.

Scripts and texts

The links between drama and English are most apparent when it comes to working with text. Encourage your students to see how a piece of writing might be performed as a piece of drama. There are various ways of working with scripts and pieces of text that can be adapted depending on the age, ability and interests of your students, or on the area of the English curriculum you wish to cover. For instance, you might do one of these.

- Take a short extract from a play (for instance *Macbeth*) and think about how to stage it in an interesting way. You could divide the class into groups, with each group performing part of the scene. You might add movement, use repetition of certain words, create an atmosphere using sound effects, lighting and costumes, and so on. See p. 80 for an idea for staging the opening scene of the witches in *Macbeth*.
- Read a piece of text, for instance a poem, and pick out the most interesting words or ideas. Develop these into a performance.
- Find a simple story and read it through. Get the children to retell the story in an unusual format. For instance, retelling *Little Red Riding Hood* as a rap.
- Get the children to write their own scripts, based around a theme you have been studying.
- Stage extracts from well-known plays. This may be a simple performance created during a single lesson, or a longer project where the students organize costumes, props, lighting, etc.

The three witches

- Working as a whole class, get three volunteers to read through the witches scene from *Macbeth* (see Appendix Three for a photocopiable version that you can use with your students).
- Talk with the class about what is happening in the extract and what kind of characters the witches are. Think about how they might say their lines. Discuss and define any unusual vocabulary, for instance 'hurlyburly'.
- Split the class into groups of three. Get the students to read the scene several times over in their groups, with one student taking each part.
- Come back together as a class to brainstorm ideas for a performance.
- Divide the class into four groups – one group for each of the witches, and one group to discuss and add sound effects.
- If there is time, ask the children to get into their groups and work together to learn their lines. Alternatively, this might be set as a homework task.
- While the witches groups are doing this, talk with the sound effects group about their ideas.
- Get each group to stand in a corner of the room.
- Practise performing the scene as a chorus – each group saying the lines together, while the fourth group add in their sound effects.
- If you have lights, costumes, etc. available, discuss with the class how these might be used.
- Perform the scene again, adding in lighting and so on.
- Talk together about the kind of atmosphere that was created.

Learning lines

At some stage in your time as a teacher of drama, it is likely that you will be asking your students to learn lines. This might involve memorizing a short piece of text for a lesson; it could be learning lots of lines for a school play. Rather than simply giving your students the text and telling them to go away and learn it, there are actually some useful tips that you can give them. The ideas below are strategies that I have developed over the years, to help me memorize scripts and other texts. You'll also see below the techniques applied to the following piece of text from the Prologue of Shakespeare's *Romeo and Juliet*.

'Two households, both alike in dignity,
In fair Verona, where we lay our scene,
From ancient grudge break to new mutiny,
Where civil blood make civil hands unclean.'

- Pick out the most important words and learn these, rather than trying to memorize everything.
   o So, in the example above, the words might be 'households', 'dignity', 'Verona', 'grudge', 'mutiny', 'civil', 'unclean'.
   o To help yourself learn these, find a way of linking them, for instance with a mnemonic or a visual set of ties.
- If the text rhymes, or has a rhythm such as iambic pentameter, this makes it much easier to learn.
   o In these instances, put a stress in your mind on the main 'beats' of the rhythm. For example, 'house', 'like', 'ty'.
   o Use the rhythm to make it more memorable, for instance singing it over and over again as a song.
   o Things tend to be more memorable where they are big or bold – when you read the piece through with rhythm, put an over-emphasis on the beats that are stressed.
- Repetition can help – if you read it through enough times, it will begin to stick.
- Once you've got most of the piece memorized, consider which bits you always seem to forget.
   o Put a particular emphasis on learning these words or phrases, finding a way to make them memorable for you. For instance, if you always forget 'grudge', then think about a really big grudge between the two households.
   o Alternatively, find a way to make the word itself memorable, for instance thinking about all the words that sound similar, such as 'trudge' and 'fudge'.

Writing in drama

There are plenty of opportunities for incorporating exciting and relevant written work into drama lessons. A word of warning, though: if time for drama is limited, it is perhaps best to stick to practical activities and leave most of the writing for homework tasks or English lessons. You might also find that your students resent spending time on writing in what they rightly see as a practical and active subject. Obviously, the higher the level of study, the greater will be the need to do written work. At GCSE and A level, being able to comment on and evaluate their drama is a vital component of the course.

Think ahead of time about the practicalities of actually doing some writing during the lesson. You will need to consider:

- What the students will write on – exercise books, loose paper, in a specific drama book.
- How you will store their writing – in folders, in books, in named drawers.
- Where the writing will be kept – in a cupboard in the drama space, in the children's work drawers in the primary classroom, on the walls as part of a display. If you are considering letting the students take books or folders away with them, how sure are you that they will remember to bring them back?
- Who will provide equipment – do you expect the students to turn up with pens, pencils, etc., or do you plan to offer these? Give plenty of advance warning if you choose the former option – students may not bring pencil cases to drama because they are not expecting to write.
- Where the students will do the writing – at desks in a classroom, on clipboards sat on the floor.
- When in the lesson the writing will take place – this will depend on the kind of writing you are doing. For instance, is it an in-role piece designed to use as part of the drama or an evaluation of work done during the lesson?

Where time is limited, make use of short, written activities that spark the imagination, drive the story onwards, or build up characterization. Here are some suggestions for written activities that fit very well into drama lessons:

- writing and performing a monologue that shows the audience more about a character.
- creating a diary entry at a specific moment in a character's life – choose a moment that is full of tension, drama or intrigue
- writing a letter to an agony aunt to bring out a character's problems and issues
- completing some kind of report, or writing a non-fiction piece, for instance a police report based on a crime scene investigation
- writing using a new technology, for example an email or a post on a website forum
- doing an evaluation of work done in a lesson – depending on their age and ability, this might be written in essay style or you might give the students an evaluation form to complete
- writing a review of a play that the class has been to see at a theatre, or perhaps of a school production.

6

Role play and characterization

In this chapter, I look at why role play is so beneficial, and at how you can encourage your children to develop their characterization skills further, as they move beyond initial role plays and into 'proper' dramatic performances. I explore the various aspects that are put together to create a realistic character, giving lots of activities for you to use. As the students develop their characterization skills, you will also want to explore the idea of relationships, and you can find more advanced ideas in this chapter about looking at gender issues, status and motivation.

Role play

At its heart, drama is all about taking on different roles. In fact, if you look at young children playing imaginary characters, often without any prompting from adults, it seems that we might be genetically predisposed to do drama. Even those primary teachers with no specialist knowledge of drama will still incorporate a role-play area or some role play into their classrooms.

Drama is all about character: what is going to happen to this person, in this situation, at this time? Seeing what happens to other people, and how they behave and feel, can be gripping and entertaining. It also helps us to put our own lives in perspective and to understand other people's viewpoints. Role play, even at its most basic, can help children develop empathy. This of course has knock-on effects in terms of social relationships both in school and beyond.

The benefits of role play

Role play has a huge range of benefits. This is recognized by the use of role-play areas in early years and some Key Stage One classrooms. When involved in role play, the children will be:

- using and enhancing their imaginative skills
- seeing what people might do in different settings and situations
- building a narrative through working from inside a story
- experiencing what it's like to be someone else
- understanding why some people behave differently to others
- seeing things from another viewpoint or perspective.

Using role plays

In the nursery and the primary school, the very first introduction to drama is often through the use of a role-play area. In fact, the majority of children will role play naturally, often choosing it as a game in the playground or the home ('let's play happy families'). At their most basic, role-play areas offer a location and perhaps some costumes and props. The children take on characters and create stories as they wish, effectively developing an improvisation, often with little or no input from the teacher. Typical scenes might include a shop, a café or a hospital.

Some primary teachers might like to develop the role-play area further. One way of doing this is to give the children an added focus for their storyline, giving them a way of creating the dramatic tension that is so often missing from schoolchildren's drama. For instance if your area is set up as a shop, and depending on the age of the children, you might add in:

- a customer making a complaint
- an accident
- a shop assistant getting sacked
- a shoplifter
- a robbery.

Facial expression

The actor's face plays a key part in creating a character and in putting across that person's moods, feelings, responses, secrets, and so on. The amount of facial expression required will vary according to the medium in which an actor is performing. In a film, naturalism is the key. The smallest changes in the face can portray a great deal about the character's inner feelings on the big screen. On stage, the face may need to be less naturalistic to get the message across or to fit in with the audience's expectations, particularly in a form such as the musical.

It is often the case that, at first, students tend to overdo their use of facial expressions. They put on an expression that they think describes an emotion, rather than allowing the feeling to come from within to create the external look. For older students studying the subject at GCSE or beyond, it can be useful to experiment with mirrors or with videotaping a series of different expressions and emotions. Below are a couple of activities designed to develop the use of facial expression.

Mirror, mirror

- *Work in pairs. Stand facing each other, as though looking into a mirror.*
- *Make a range of big facial expressions, with one person copying the other. You might yawn wide, stick out your tongue or frown for example.*
- *Swap over so that the other person gets a go at leading.*
- *Once you've warmed your faces up, try making a range of facial expressions to express emotion – happy, sad, disappointed. Again, mirror the expressions made by your partner.*

Freeze-frame moods

- *Work in small groups of about four or five.*
- *Between you, decide on a mood that you are going to portray.*
- *Create a freeze-frame that shows this mood.*
- Looking at each group in turn, try to guess each mood.

Voice

Voice obviously plays a key role in portraying a character. Encourage your students to do plenty of observations of the way in which different people use their voices. In a secondary school, you might ask them to consider the voices of different teachers, and the kind of messages their voice sends about them. In a primary school, you could ask the children to think about the voices of the various staff in the school, from the head to the caretaker.

It's essential for an actor to use his or her voice properly and not to stress or strain it. After all without a voice, there can be no performance (unless of course you're doing a mime or movement piece). Effective voice usage is equally important for teachers – you only have one voice and you can't get a new one if you damage it or wear it out. If you get the chance, it really is worth doing some voice training and learning some vocal exercises to improve your voice usage.

Breath and posture

In order to speak and project effectively, it's vital for an actor to use his or her breathing correctly. A key part of learning to breathe and speak well is about understanding how to adopt and maintain a good posture. From the youngest age, encourage your children to hold their bodies properly – it will obviously help them in drama but it will be equally beneficial in lessons where they must sit and write. A good posture helps develop muscular tone and guards against back, neck and shoulder problems in later life.

The Alexander Technique is a well-known approach for developing good posture and overcoming voice problems. It is used by actors, dancers, singers and many others. It was created by F.M. Alexander, an actor who experienced vocal problems and who, as a consequence, developed his own 'technique' for overcoming muscular tension. The best way of learning the technique is through one-to-one lessons with a qualified teacher. In my first career as a dancer, I learnt the Alexander Technique to overcome chronic back problems, and can highly recommend it. For more information, see www.stat.org.uk.

Posture and breathing exercise
Practise this exercise, using the instructions below, before guiding your students through it.

- Stand in a space with your arms relaxed by your side, feet directly under your hips, knees slightly bent.
- Breathe in and out without forcing it, gradually becoming aware of where the breath is coming from in your body.
- As you breathe in, you should feel your diaphragm expanding, as you breathe out it should fall back in.
- Aim to breathe in through your nose and out through your mouth.
- Breathe in for a count of two then out for a count of three. (Many people over breathe or hyperventilate, particularly when they are tense, and will find it counter-intuitive to do this.) If you feel dizzy at any point, you should stop.
- Now think about the muscular tension in your body, and about adopting a good posture.
- Imagine there is a string tied to the back of your head. Feel the string pulling you gently upwards, like a puppet, with your chin tilting very slightly down and your neck lengthening.
- Lift your shoulders up to your ears then drop them down, feeling all the tension release.
- Now become conscious of what your arms are doing. Are they slightly bent? If they are, try to release the tension in your elbows so that your arms fall straight.
- Move down to your hands. Clench them into fists and then release them. Feel the tension dropping out of your fingers.
- Next become aware of what your hips are doing. Release any tension and rock your hips slightly so that this area relaxes.
- Move down to your knees, ensuring that they are slightly bent and fully relaxed.
- Finally, think about how your feet feel on the floor. Imagine that you are fully rooted to the ground, with all parts of the foot touching it, and gravity keeping you safely secured.

Volume

The ability to project the voice is clearly crucial for live theatre, because it allows the audience to hear what we are saying. It's obviously important for teachers as well, although it's very easy to get into bad vocal habits. Many teachers will make too much use of a loud volume and too little use of a very quiet one (and I include myself in that comment). Try the following activities to get both you and your students thinking about volume and the effect it has on those listening.

One to ten

- Standing in a space, count slowly as a class from one to ten.
- Start very quietly, gradually getting louder as you count upwards.
- 'One' should be almost whispering, 'ten' should be almost shouting.
- Afterwards, talk about how this felt. *What does a louder volume feel like? What kind of character might speak quietly or loudly?*

Ten to one

- Repeat the exercise, but this time in the opposite direction.
- Start at ten (very loud) and count backwards to one (very quiet).
- This is a great activity to try on an INSET day with teaching staff. It demonstrates how quietly you can speak, yet still be heard by the students. It also shows how talking more quietly forces the children to listen more carefully.

Back off

- This is a whole-class exercise.
- Divide the class into two.
- Each half of the class should form a line down the middle of the room, so that the two lines are facing each other.
- You are going to recite the nursery rhyme 'Baa Baa Black

Sheep' (or similar). *Every time I [the teacher] bang the drum, take one step backwards, away from the line opposite you.*

− *As you move further away from each other, project your voice more but don't shout.*
− *Imagine that your voice is a ball that you are throwing towards the other person.*

Tone

The tone of your voice can reveal a great deal about how you are feeling inside. In fact, *how* a character says something can often reveal more than *what* they actually say, especially where there is a secret or subtext involved. The exercises below will encourage your students to play around with tone. There's a lot to be said for teachers using as much tone as possible as well − it can be very useful in managing a class.

Number quarrel

− *Work in pairs. The aim is to develop your use of tone.*
− *Have a quarrel with each other, using only consecutive numbers.*
− *You can say as many or as few numbers as you like.*
− *For instance, the first person says '1, 2, 3', the second says '4, 5', the third says '6' and so on.*
− Listen to performances from a few volunteers.
− *Can we tell what they are 'saying'? How is it possible for us to understand without words?* Highlight the use of tone and body language.
− *Now repeat the quarrel, this time using words. Aim to keep the same level of tone in the voice.*

Pronunciation

Some children have clear voices and excellent pronunciation. Other children really struggle to make themselves understood. Drama can help a great deal in encouraging students to speak properly and to enunciate their words. Try the activities given below as a vocal warm-up, or as a fun starter activity.

A to Z

- Say the alphabet out loud together with your class, talking slowly.
- The students should speak in a greatly exaggerated manner, making large movements with their mouths, lips, faces, etc. as they say each letter.

Soft letters, sharp letters

- Practise pronouncing the different letters of the alphabet with your class.
- Start with some soft-sounding letters: c, f, s, z.
- Move on to some hard-sounding letters: d, k, p, t.
- Ask the children to think about how they form the sounds. What are they doing with their:
  - mouth
  - lips
  - tongue
  - teeth?

Mouth at work

- Practise the letter sounds that make particular use of the lips.
- For instance: b, m, o, p.
- Now practise the sounds that are formed with the tongue and teeth.
- For example: d, l, n, t, w.
- Finally, practise the vowel sounds, thinking about how each one is formed and over-exaggerating the mouth movements required.

Tongue-twisters

- Practise saying tongue twisters – they're a great way to get your students moving their mouths and practising pronunciation. They're also a lot of fun.
- Try this link for a list of tongue-twisters and also some audio files to use with your students: www.teachingenglish.org.uk/download/audio/twist/twist.shtml.

Excuse me?

- *Work with a partner.*
- *Choose a topic for your conversation.*
- *While you talk, one of you has a fit of:*
  - o *yawning*
  - o *sneezing*
  - o *coughing*
  - o *burping*
  - o *hiccupping*
  - o *laughing.*
- *Try to keep focused in your character.*
- *Once you've had a go, swap roles and try again.*
- *What happened to your pronunciation during this exercise?*

A thought on accents and dialects

Personally, I would encourage your students to steer clear of using accents or dialects, unless they are very talented at doing it. Done badly an accent can be unintentionally hilarious. Some teachers seem to have a very good ear for the way that others speak, and might consciously or subconsciously mirror the way their students talk. Where this is done subtly, it can help a teacher bond with the class.

Dialogue

It's surprisingly hard to write or improvise realistic dialogue. Often, what we end up with is a clichéd version of normal speech. Clearly, simply recreating a realistic conversation on the stage could potentially be very dull. Encourage your children to find a balance between what people might actually say, and the kind of dialogue that is interesting and engaging for an audience.

Listening in

- *Work individually in a space. You are giving only one half of a conversation. We don't hear what the other person is saying.*

- *Imagine you are talking to someone and are . . .*
  o *ending a relationship.*
  o *feeling very depressed.*
  o *talking to a small child.*
  o *trying to calm down an angry crowd.*
  o *an angry customer.*

What's my line? (1)

- Work in small groups of about four people.
- Give each group around four bits of dialogue written on slips of paper. Use the same snippets for each group. For instance, you might use:
  o 'Quick! Let's go! There's no time to waste.'
  o 'I don't believe it – she's dead!'
  o 'Did you hear that noise?'
  o 'What the hell are you doing?'
- Create a planned improvisation using all four lines.
- Watch the groups perform their improvisations. *Were the stories similar or different and why?*
- *Did different groups use the same dialogue lines in different ways?*

What's my line? (2)

- Again, work in small groups of around four students.
- This time, give one line only to one member of each group. This person should keep the line secret.
- Give the class a setting/scenario, for instance a family quarrel or a bank robbery.
- The person with the line must somehow get it into the improvisation, sounding as natural as possible.
- At the end, the rest of the group have to guess what was written on the slip of paper.

Back-to-back

- *Working in pairs, stand with your backs together.*
- *Improvise a telephone conversation with a friend. Do not look around at each other – focus only on the dialogue.*

- *Now try again, this time adding in some pauses. During each pause, take it in turns to say an 'aside' to the audience.*
- If necessary, explain to the class that an 'aside' is a line spoken directly to the audience by a character. In the context of a phone call, it's the kind of thing they might say with their hand over the receiver so that the person at the other end can't hear.
- Talk with the class about the kind of things that might be said in an aside, and the effect that it has on the audience.

Collecting conversation

- This makes a useful homework task.
- Ask the students to spend a week collecting some snippets of dialogue that they overhear.
- These might be gathered on the bus, at home, in the park, etc.
- They should write the more interesting snippets down, and bring them into class.
- Some of the snippets could be used to develop into improvisations.

Body language

In drama (and indeed in real life), the body can say as much as the voice. Our body language is often sending subconscious messages about how we feel, perhaps without us being aware that this is happening. Teachers are, of course, only too aware of this fact. At the same time, we are constantly making judgements about others, depending on what their bodies are telling us. The way that a class reacts to a teacher, particularly one whom the students don't know well, is at least partly based on the strength and quality of his or her body language.

The body language used to portray different characters will vary according to age, personality, occupation, situation, emotion, and so on. Learning how to adapt their body language to fit a particular person will play a key role in how realistic your students' characterisations are.

You'll find a couple of exercises on the next page designed to get your children thinking about how to use body language in a more inventive and creative way.

Mood statues

- *Stand in a space. On the first drum beat, start to move around the room. As you walk, think of a mood – sad, happy, furious, depressed, joyful.*
- *On the second drum beat freeze, showing the mood you thought of through your face and body.*
- Pick out about five students who are doing this particularly well. They remain frozen in position like statues.
- Everyone else unfreezes, walking around the space to 'visit' each of the mood statues.
- Try to identify what the different moods are, talking about how and why the statue positions are effective.

The animal bus

- Set up 12 chairs in two blocks of six, as though they are pairs of seats on a bus.
- Ask for about eight volunteers to perform an improvisation.
- Each actor should choose an animal. They could do this as a group or individually.
- The performers are going to use the animals to inform their characters. They should stand and move in a way that echoes the animal they have chosen, while still retaining a realistic human character.
- So, a giraffe might walk slowly with a very upright posture, while a snake would move smoothly and sinuously.
- Begin the improvisation. The characters can get on and off as they wish. As on a real bus, they will probably not do much talking.
- When the improvisation has finished, talk about how the characters behaved, and the kinds of animals that they brought to mind.
- Repeat the exercise in small groups of about six to eight students.

Age

Looking at how people move, speak and behave at different ages is a great way of building characterization skills. The contrasts between a young and an old person tend to be quite graphic. Consequently, they are reasonably easy for children to portray. Many young people will be in regular contact with their grandparents or younger siblings, and will be able to tell you all about the differences that age can bring. We can have a fairly fixed view of what young and old people are like and it is interesting to challenge any stereotypes or preconceptions that your children might hold. The exercises that follow will encourage your students to develop characters using age as a factor in their performances.

The cycle of life

- This exercise is a great starter activity for work on this theme.
- If offers a good way to get your students thinking about how we behave at different ages, and looking at the circular nature of life.
- The activity is done individually, although there are moments when the students can interact.
- The children should mime rather than talk, so that they can hear what you are saying throughout.
- You might bang a drum to indicate when each stage is finished.
- Talk the class through the ageing process, from birth to death, as follows.
- *First, lie on your side in a space, curled up like a foetus.*
- *You have just been born. You are a tiny baby just come into the world.*
- *Now you are nine months old and you are just learning to crawl.*
- *You're a year old now, and you are pulling up and just beginning to walk. You keep falling over but you carry on trying.*
- *Now you're five and it's playtime on your first day at school. You look around at the other children. Maybe you decide to go up to someone else and talk with them; perhaps you prefer to keep to yourself.*
- *You're older now, eleven, and it's your first day at secondary school. You're trying to look cool and confident, but inside you feel scared.*

- *It's your leaving day at school, and you are attending the school disco. You get yourself ready to go out (you might do this individually or in a small group). When you arrive at the disco you're very excited – you feel like a grown up at last.*
- *Now you've left school and you're going for an interview for a new job. As you arrive, you feel nervous but excited. There are lots of other people around, all waiting and competing for the same job. Do you try to make friends with them or do you keep yourself apart?*
- *You're older now, and you have just become a parent for the first time. Imagine you are holding your new baby in your arms. Look at your baby – how do you feel about bringing a new life into the world?*
- *Now you're getting much older. You've become a grandparent and you have taken your grandchild to the park for the day. As you play together, the differences in age become apparent.*
- *You're nearing the end of your life now, and feeling very stiff and old. It's hard for you to move. You go to lie down on your bed for a rest, and gradually fall asleep for the very last time.*

Memories

- *Work in pairs. Put two chairs together, to make a bench.*
- *Improvise, using the following scenario.*
- *You are two old men, who happen to sit on the same park bench.*
- *You get chatting and realize that you knew each other years ago. You reminisce about the 'good old days'.*
- After a few minutes, as the class to freeze.
- Tell the pairs they are now going to flash back, improvising a scene from when their characters knew each other before. For instance, at school, at a party, in the war.
- The students should show clearly the difference in the way that the characters moved when they were younger.
- Get the class to freeze again. Bring the improvisation back to the present day.

The visit

- *Work in pairs. One of you is a young person, the other a grand- parent.*

- *The young person is visiting his or her grandparent.*
- *Add some interest to the scene: for instance, the grandparent is very moody, or the young person doesn't really want to be there.*
- *Again, focus on the difference in the way that the characters move, speak, and so on.*

The old people's home

- *You will be working as a whole class to create an improvisation based in an old people's home.*
- *Some of you will play the old people, some will be their carers, others will play visitors – family, friends, etc.*
- *As a class, decide on the format of the improvisation. Will it be a fairly quiet, flat scene, or will something sudden or shocking happen?*

Occupation

The job that a person does will, of course, affect the way that the character should be portrayed. Children seem to enjoy using occupation as a basis for creating a character. With younger children, the performance might be rather stereotyped, but it still gives a good way into being someone else. Add hats, costumes or props if you can, to engage your students more fully. You will find some activities below, based around people's occupations.

What's my job?

- Ask for volunteers to mime different occupations to the class.
- Guess what the job is from watching the performance, for instance:
  - police officer
  - gardener
  - musician
  - scientist
  - firefighter.
- *How did we know what the person's job was?*

The status gap

- *Work in pairs.*
- Give the students a pair of occupations where there is a gulf in the status between the two characters. For example:
  - ○ doctor and patient
  - ○ teacher and pupil
  - ○ king and servant
  - ○ boss and secretary.
- *Improvise a scene involving the two characters.*
- Look at some performances.
- Talk about how the gap in status is reflected in the way that the people behave.

The goalkeeper

- *Work individually, standing in a space of your own.*
- *Imagine you are a goalkeeper.*
- *Mime the progress of the game that is taking place at the other end of the pitch.*
- *Use your face and body to show high points (your team score a goal) and low points (your striker misses a clear chance to score).*

Relationships

The relationship between two or more characters can create some very interesting material for drama, particularly where there is some kind of conflict involved. Relationships give depth to the drama by allowing for the creation of subtext or dramatic irony (see p. 121 and p. 124). For instance, one character might either:

- despise the other
- be secretly in love with the other
- be angry with the other
- be taking care of the other
- want to persuade the other to do something.

To create tension, use situations in which at least one of the characters would be cross or angry with another. For instance, with the student working in pairs, ask them to improvise one of these scenes.

- *You borrowed a dress from your sister without asking, and accidentally ruined it. She has just come across it in her wardrobe and wants to know what has happened. She's not happy.*
- *You're in a minor car crash. You and the other driver both get out of your cars. You argue as to whose fault the crash was.*
- *You and a younger sibling are sitting watching TV. You start to argue over which channel to watch.*
- *You've had a hairdo and you're not happy with it.*
- *You're given the wrong change in a shop.*

Situations in which one character must persuade another about something can provide useful material. This is especially so where the person is not going to be easily persuaded. Here are some suggestions for improvisations around this theme.

- A salesperson tries to sell a pointless gadget to a customer.
- A hairdresser suggests a customer should 'try the latest style'.
- Your football lands in the garden of a moody neighbour, and you want to get it back.
- You need to borrow your bus fare from a stranger.
- 'Will you marry me?'
- You're late, and must come up with an original excuse to persuade your teacher not to punish you.

Schooldays
Try this whole-class improvisation to explore how our relationships in the school setting change over time.

- *Stand in a space on your own. Close your eyes.*
- *Imagine it is your first ever day at school. How do you feel? What are you thinking? What kind of person are you? Will you find it easy or hard to make friends?*
- *When I say 'go', all go straight into an improvisation of 'the first day*

at school', based in the school playground just after the parents have dropped the children off.

- Run the improvisation for a short time, then freeze the students.
- *Again, close your eyes. Now think back to your first day at secondary school. How did you feel? What were your fears, concerns and hopes? Did your friends come to the same school? If not, how did you hope to make new ones?*
- Again, run the improvisation for a few minutes, this time based in a school assembly hall where the head teacher will shortly be giving a talk.
- Finally, repeat the exercise but this time with the first day in a sixth form, based in the sixth-form common room.
- After the students have done the improvisations, talk with them about the differences between the relationships in each one.

Gender

There are lots of interesting exercises that you can do to look at the differences between men and women, and also at how the two genders might interact with each other. Many of these exercises will bring up issues of stereotyping, and this can lead on to some useful discussion work. In a single-sex school, it is perhaps particularly important to explore gender issues and the characterization of men and women. Of course, if you are teaching in a single-sex environment, it will be vital for the sake of your school drama productions that the students do learn how to portray the opposite gender in a realistic way.

Depending on the prevailing attitudes of your students and in your school, you might find it hard to persuade them to take on a character of the opposite gender. And when a boy does play a girl, or vice versa, this can be the source of much embarrassment/ridicule/silliness/amusement. In the prevailing climate in some of our schools, it can be particularly tricky for boys to play girls. What is needed is a feeling of consideration and respect within the class, and a teacher with high expectations of the behaviour and attitudes of his or her students.

The first few times you try changing gender roles, you could stick to individual activities (as in 'Going on a date' and 'The dating agency' below). At this stage you may wish to be reasonably accepting of some low-level silliness. This should gradually lessen as the students become more used to taking on different roles. Alternatively, you may find that there is absolutely no fuss at all, particularly with younger, primary-aged children. The activities below will help you explore the different ways in which the two genders can be portrayed.

Going on a date

- *Work individually, sitting in a space on a chair.*
- *You are a girl, getting ready for a date.*
- *You might be putting on make up, doing your hair, choosing clothes from your wardrobe.*
- Continue the improvisation for a few minutes.
- *Now try it again, this time playing a boy.*
- Afterwards, talk about the differences between the two performances. *Did we stereotype the characters? How realistic were they?*

The dating agency

This exercise works just like a monologue. You might like to video the end results, or simply ask for volunteers to show what they have done to the class.

- *You've come to a dating agency.*
- *You could be divorced or single, male or female.*
- *You are going to make a one-minute video about yourself.*
- *You need to 'sell' yourself to potential dates.*

First date

- *Work in pairs.*
- *It's your first date. Decide on a venue (the cinema, a walk in the park).*
- *You don't know each other well at all.*

- *Show how awkward you feel through what your characters say and do.*

The interview

- *Work in small groups.*
- *One person is the boss, the others are interviewees coming for a job as a secretary.*
- *The boss is extremely sexist and is more interested in looks than in qualifications.*
- First time round the boss is male, the interviewees are female. Ask students to try out the improvisation.
- Now swap the roles over, so that the boss is female and the interviewees are male.
- After the improvisations, talk about your experience of the situations with different genders.
- This activity could lead well into work on status (see below).

Status

The term status describes where one character stands in relation to another, i.e. their relative importance. Status is very subjective. If you were a big football fan, you would probably feel that famous football players have very high status. If you met a famous footballer you would probably feel overawed and impressed. However, if you had no interest in football, and had no idea who the famous person was, you would not confer status on him simply for what he does.

There are many different things that can confer status on a person, such as these.

- Gender: although things are changing in many societies, historically men have often been given much more automatic status than women.
- Job: a high court judge is generally accepted to have a high-status profession; a cleaner is normally viewed as a low-status job.

- Social position: a queen would have more status than her servant.
- Age: a young child is generally viewed as having less status than his or her parents, although this perception has changed considerably over the last 50 or so years.
- Personality: the most confident person within a group might 'take over' and become a leader. Other more confident members would consequently be given status by the other less confident members.
- Situation: at school, a difficult student might have high status among his or her peers – while at home, the same child could have very low status.
- Group: a student who is a brilliant footballer could have high status in the football team – but low status in the classroom.

Here are some drama exercises that will help your students to understand what status is and how it works.

Playing card status
This exercise works well with about half a class at a time. There are various ways of doing it – I've explained two possible options below.

- Hand out playing cards to about 12 to 15 students.
- Aim for a good spread of cards, e.g. from 2 through to Ace (I normally say that Ace is high, although you could also make the King the highest card).

Now you can either follow this set of instructions.

- The students look at their cards to see what status they have (e.g. 7 is middle status, Queen is high status).
- They move around the room, relating to the other students, in the way denoted by their status (e.g. a Queen would walk around with a snooty expression and be dismissive of other people).
- The other half of the class watches. Their aim is to work out the relative order of status.

- After a few minutes, the audience must line up the students in order of status.
- The students then hold up their cards to check how well the audience did.
- The two halves of the class swap over and have another go.

Or, alternatively, you can follow this set.

- The students do not look at their cards but hold them against their foreheads instead, with them facing outwards so that everyone else can see them.
- They move around the room, responding to others according to the number of the status card held against that person's head.
- At the end of the time, the students line themselves up according to what they believe is the number of their card. They judge this by how other people treated them.
- Did they get it right? If not, why not?

Status pairings

- *There are plenty of pairings that have a good contrast in status.*
- *Think of real-life situations where one person has much more control than another.*
- For instance:
  o brother and sister, where one sibling is much older or more aggressive than the other
  o parent and child, particularly in the past – the further in the past, the more likely the status is to differ in favour of the parent
  o man and woman – again, if the setting is an historical one there will be an obvious difference
  o guard and prisoner – the status gap will be greater depending on the personalities of the two characters.

Outside the head's office
Students are typically very aware of the different status levels within the school. They seem to understand that some children

have more power within their peer group than others, sometimes irrespective of their chronological age. This tag improvisation takes advantage of this fact.

- Put a line of chairs at the front of the room (about four or five is right).
- *Imagine the chairs are located outside the head teacher's office.*
- Talk about how some students are sent to the head's office for good reasons (to show an excellent piece of work), while others are sent for bad reasons (to deal with serious misbehaviour).
- As students think of a character, they enter the improvisation.
- Set a maximum for the number of people on stage at a time (about four works well).
- A new character can only enter when another person leaves.
- Let the improvisation develop.
- Afterwards, talk about the varying levels of status and why it was that some characters were more powerful than others.

Motive and motivation

Whatever we do, there will always be a motive or a motivation for us doing it. Sometimes, the motive is very simple – a child might share his crisps with a friend in the hope of getting some chocolate in return. Often, though, our motives are more complex. For instance, we are motivated to turn up to work every day because we get paid. But for many jobs, including teaching, our job is about much more than that. Additional motives might include a desire to make a difference, an intrinsic love of what we do, a sense of vocation.

As students get older, they will be better able to understand the complexities of this idea – that a character might have various motives for what he or she does, and that this might influence the way that the person behaves. Often, when we examine a character's motivation, moral issues are brought to the fore. You can introduce your students to this concept by using the following activities.

You're being followed

- *Work in pairs. Stand in a space, one a little distance behind the other.*
- *On the first drum beat, follow your partner around the room, staying a few feet apart.*
- *On the second drum beat, freeze.*
- *Now think of a reason why you are following your partner. For instance, you might:*
  - *need to ask for directions*
  - *be intending to mug them*
  - *be a stalker*
  - *want to get the person's autograph because they are famous*
  - *have picked up a bag that the person has forgotten and be intending to hand it back.*
- *On the third drum beat continue walking, this time with your motivation in mind. How might it influence the way that your character behaves? If you wish, you can try to catch up with your partner.*
- Repeat several times, using a range of motivations.
- *Talk together with your partner about how the exercise felt for each of you.*

What I'm really thinking

- *Work in small groups of about six.*
- Give the students a scenario in which one person is presenting to, addressing or teaching, the others. For instance, to
  - a primary school class
  - a chat show
  - a church service.
- In each group, the person doing the presentation needs a 'sidekick'. This person is going to voice his or her unspoken thoughts.
- *Develop an improvisation in which every time the presenter says something (Priest: 'It's lovely to see you all here for Midnight Mass'), the sidekick voices his or her real thoughts ('Considering I never see you the rest of year').*

Joyrider

- This exercise uses the 'judgement chair' format (see p. 24–5 for more details).
- One volunteer sits in the chair. This person plays a teenage joyrider who has crashed a car and killed the two friends who were passengers.
- The other students come up and address the joyrider, taking on various characters.
- For example, they might play:
  o the parents of the dead friends
  o the police
  o the joyrider's parents
  o a social worker
  o a journalist.
- Each time, they should consider what their motive is for addressing the joyrider. What do they want to get out of the situation? For instance, do they want to make the person feel guilty, to protect the joyrider, to get a good story to sell more newspapers, etc?

7

Dramatic tension

In this chapter, I explore the idea of adding dramatic tension to drama, giving lots of ideas about why and how this should be done. You'll find out about what dramatic tension actually is, and why it's so important in creating effective drama. You'll also find a range of ways in which you can encourage your students to add more dramatic tension to their performances, with lots of activities and exercises to show how this can be done.

What is tension?

Tension often comes about when we feel under pressure to do or not do something. We might be overloaded with work, under psychological pressure to conform, or tempted to have a cigarette when we've given up. Try the following activity to get your students thinking about what tension is and how it makes us feel.

- *Think about something which happened to you recently that made you feel tense, for instance the build-up to an exam.*
- *What was it about the situation that made you feel tense? How did it make you feel physically? How did it make you feel emotionally?*
- *Stand on your own in a space. Tense up your face, hold it for three seconds, then release.*

- *Repeat this with each part of the body in turn, starting at the top and working downwards.*
- *Focus on one part of the body in more detail. Face – forehead, eyes shut, eyes open, teeth clenched, etc.*
- *Which parts of your body have the most tension in them?*

Laughter provides a great release from tension. You might have noticed that your students will often laugh when a performance goes wrong. This is because it's a great way of relieving the pressure and saying 'we're not taking it seriously, we don't really feel tense'. Students need to learn not to laugh at their own mistakes, and to keep going *in character* regardless of what happens. This is one of the fundamental aspects of a good performance.

Dramatic tension

The use of dramatic tension is often what makes the difference between a mediocre piece of classroom drama, and a highly charged and engaging piece. Left to their own devices, children will often tell a story that has very little tension in it. It's up to us as teachers to show them how to add dramatic tension to the mix. Many students are surprised by just what a different this makes to the overall quality of their performances.

What is dramatic tension?

Dramatic tension is obviously slightly different to the kind of tension we might feel if we are stressed at work, not least because it is not actually real. The tension comes out of the drama itself, whether as a result of what is happening, the kind of special effects that are being used, what the characters are doing, and so on. Talk with your students about how dramatic tension works, relating it to the drama that they see in their daily lives:

- *What TV programmes can you think of that are tense?*
- *Why do they make you (the audience) feel this way?*
- *What things are in these programmes that create tension?*

- *What is the effect of tension on your viewing habits? Does it make you more likely to continue watching? Why is this?*

Tension in drama is typically like a wire being stretched tighter and tighter until it snaps. There is a sense of build-up (think of the opening music in the film *Jaws*), with the tension getting higher and higher until it reaches a climax and is then resolved.

Why is dramatic tension so important?

Now ask your students to think about why dramatic tension is needed in a piece of drama. It is mainly used as a device for keeping the audience involved and engaged in the story – in effect, for keeping them watching. The audience might feel:

- desperate to know what happens next
- fascinated to see how and whether the story resolves itself
- engrossed by the situation between two characters in conflict
- an urge to call out to the characters – 'don't go in there!'

Creating dramatic tension

There are many different ways in which dramatic tension can be created. These range from how the characters behave, to the kind of situations we place them in. If you have the resources available, a lot of tension can be created by adding special effects to the drama. The sections below will give you plenty of ideas for creating more dramatic tension in your drama lessons.

Body language

Our bodies can help us show the tension that a character feels, both through the way we stand and also how we move. Often, it is the small and subtle postures and movements that will have the most impact. Stillness can have a great deal of impact where we understand the characters' inner feelings. Silence, particularly when it is a deliberate or forced silence between two or more characters, can

111

really make an audience feel on edge. Teach your students to downplay their body language, keeping it small and subtle, rather than creating melodramatic characterizations.

Being followed

− *Move around the room, as though you are walking home from school.*
− *Start off walking slowly then gradually speed up, as though you are being followed.*
− *What happens to the way you move as the sense of tension increases?*
− *What is the effect on the overall atmosphere in the room?*
− *What kind of movements did your character make? How did these movements add to the tension?*

The angry circle

− Sit the class in a circle.
− Place three chairs in the centre of the circle.
− Select three volunteers.
− The volunteers come into the space and leave it as if they are very angry with each other. They may enter and leave as they wish, coming back into the space as they like.
− No speaking is allowed − all the anger must be created through the body language and facial expressions.
− Afterwards, discuss the exercise.
− *What did they do to show us they were angry?*
− *How does the tension make the 'audience' of the rest of the class feel?*
− *How did you, the actors, feel during the scene?* Encourage them to be honest: they may well have felt an urge to laugh, as a release from tension.

Atmosphere

There are plenty of elements that can help to create a tense atmosphere in a dramatic piece, and consequently add to the dramatic tension in the performance. Many films, especially those in the horror, science fiction and ghost genres, will use special effects and other techniques to create a heightened sense of atmosphere and tension. Use the following exercise to explore how atmosphere and tension can be created on the big screen, and how this might be translated into a classroom situation.

Film clips

- Choose a film with lots of atmosphere that most of your class will have seen.
- If possible, show them a short clip of a particularly atmospheric part of the film.
- Talk together about the elements in the film that help create an atmosphere. This will typically include the areas listed below.
- Sound effects, for instance:
  o quiet, creepy sounds
  o the contrast between silence and then a sudden loud noise
  o fearful human sounds such as heavy breathing
  o weather-related sound effects, particularly the wind
  o sounds which are not quite human.
- Light and dark, for example:
  o unusual shadows
  o flickering lights that suddenly go out
  o naked flames – candlelight, oil lamps, the shadows these create
  o mist and fog – anything that means we cannot see clearly
  o a character goes into a room, the light switch doesn't work.
- Music, for instance:
  o a slow piece which gradually gets faster (think *Jaws* again)
  o an instrument playing a single note over and over again
  o sudden increases in volume
  o the sound of certain instruments, for instance the violin.
- The characters, and what they do:
  o a person alone, in the woods, at night
  o someone entering a house where a criminal might be hiding (see also dramatic irony on p. 124)

     o a person who is behaving very strangely, or who has some kind of superhuman powers

     o a lonely setting (the train platform at night) – a stranger approaches.

After you've done an analysis of how filmmakers create atmosphere, talk with your students about how they might recreate some of these elements in their own drama work.

Characters and relationships

Any time two or more people are put together in a scenario, there is a huge potential for creating dramatic tension. Of course, a great source of dramatic tension is the conflict between two characters who do not like each other. However, there can also be much tension in a situation where you feel that you must tell a friend something difficult. For instance, that you have fallen in love with her boyfriend, or that her haircut really doesn't suit her. There is also much potential for dramatic tension when we are not sure about who a character is, or what his or her intentions might be.

    Below are a few suggestions for improvisations in which the relationship between the characters helps to create dramatic tension.

I can't go out tonight

- *Work in groups of three, naming yourselves A, B and C.*
- *Do an improvisation in which A telephones B, but B says he or she 'can't go out tonight'. A few moments later C rings B, and B agrees to go out with him or her.*
- *While they are out together, A sees B and C together.*
- *What happens next?*

Alphabet quarrel

- *Working in pairs, have an alphabet quarrel, where each sentence begins with the next letter of the alphabet.*

- For instance, 'Anyway . . .', 'But . . .', 'Come on . . .', 'Don't be an idiot . . .', 'Every time . . .'.
- Try and sustain or hopefully build the tension between the two characters as you quarrel.
- See if you can get to the end of the alphabet – you can cheat on X if you want to, by using words that start with an X sound ('ecstatic', 'excited').

The hitchhiker from hell

- Work in pairs.
- Set up a 'car' – two chairs side by side.
- In this improvisation you pick up a hitchhiker. At first, all seems well. You chat together about this and that.
- After a while, you begin to feel a bit awkward. You sense that there is something not quite right about the person. You try to drop the hitchhiker off, giving a reasonable excuse, but he or she refuses to get out.
- Silence falls. You turn on the radio. A news report comes on about an escaped convict who is potentially very dangerous.
- Aim to build the tension through silence and stillness, letting it bubble up over time rather than feeling the need to force it through action.
- After everyone has tried the improvisation, look at a couple of performances.
- Talk as a class about what created the dramatic tension in the improvisations.

Confined spaces

Getting your characters stuck or confined in a small space is a great way of creating instant dramatic tension. Where space is tight, tensions between people soon build up, especially if there are issues in their relationships, or if there is an added problem to overcome. Think of how you feel when you enter a lift with someone you don't know – there is this inevitable feeling of awkwardness, which is only dissipated when the doors open and one or other of you gets out. Below are some exercises that use a lack of space to create dramatic tension.

Trapped!

- *Work in a small group of about four or five people.*
- *Define a tight space with four chairs, just big enough to fit all of you in.*
- *The chairs are going to represent various tight spaces.*
- Choose a suitable setting and scenario. Here are some ideas.
  - You're in a lift which gets stuck between floors.
  - You're trapped in a cave by a rock fall.
  - You're a large family driving on holiday in a small car.
- Explain to the students the scenario/setting they are to 'go' and that, when you say, they are to move straight into an improvisation.

Trapped! with a twist

- *Now repeat the improvisation, this time see how adding an additional problem will create more tension. Choose one of these.*
  - *You're in a lift which gets stuck between floors – one of you is pregnant and starts having contractions.*
  - *You're trapped in a cave by a rockfall – the torches all get smashed, and you're stuck in total darkness.*
  - *You're a large family driving on holiday in a small car – you get stuck in a traffic jam and the youngest child needs to go to the toilet.*

Tunnel trouble

- *Work in small groups – about three to five people.*
- *Set up a line of five chairs.*
- *One of you is drunk, the rest of you are typical commuters.*
- *You're travelling on the tube – get on, one at a time, and establish your characters.*
- *The train gets stuck in a tunnel. What happens next? Try to develop the tension.*
- *It's hard to do this exercise well. The temptation is to overplay it, particularly the drunk. Instead, aim to use awkward silences and body language to create the tension.*

A series of problems

Another very effective way to create tension is to come up with a series of problems that your character or characters must solve. The problems gradually become worse and worse until they reach a climactic moment of awfulness! This approach has been used in many films, such as *Speed* and *Titanic*. The audience is kept hooked, because they are wondering 'what on earth will happen *next?*' This technique is relatively easy for your students to use, and offers them a good way of adding tension to a performance. Try the activity below to show them how this approach creates dramatic tension.

The boat trip

- *Work in small groups of about four to six people.*
- *You are a group (schoolchildren, tourists, etc.) who are going out on a boat trip.*
- *As the boat trip progresses, various problems occur, rising in danger each time.*
- You might go straight into the improvisation and see what happens, or plan the series of problems first and then try it out.
- Your series of problems could be like this.
  o Someone has a stomach-ache.
  o You've forgotten the packed lunches.
  o Someone begins to get seasick.
  o A quarrel brews up.
  o You're lost and have forgotten the map.
  o The sea starts to get choppy.
  o Someone falls over board.
  o A storm begins to rage.
  o The boat starts to sink.
  o There are no life jackets.
  o The boat sinks.
  o The sharks arrive!
- You can do the same exercise in various different settings, preferably ones where the characters are unable to easily escape (for instance, on a plane or a train).

Suspense

Suspense is perhaps best described as the feeling that something is 'about to happen'. For the audience, the dramatic tension comes about because they are not quite sure whether that something will actually happen or not. They are literally 'suspended' and uncertain of what the outcome will be. Here are some ideas for exciting, suspenseful scenarios to use with your class.

- *You're a team of bomb disposal experts in the middle of defusing a bomb.*
- *You're locked out of your house and you left a pan boiling on the cooker inside.*
- *A meteorite is going to hit Earth in the next few minutes.*
- *A robbery has gone wrong, one of your gang has been shot, and the police are on their way.*

Conflict

Conflict, whether verbal, psychological or physical, is perhaps the simplest way of creating dramatic tension. In fact, it's often what students turn to immediately to 'spice up' a piece of drama if it's feeling a bit dull. With younger students, play fights can become a bit of an irritant for the drama teacher. In the middle of an improvisation, a fight will kick off and the students will tussle with each other, often ending the piece in fits of laughter. Although this might be funny for those involved, it is rarely particularly interesting for the audience.

Consequently, when exploring conflict, particularly the physical kind, you should make it clear to your class how difficult it is to make fighting an interesting part of a drama. You might go so far as to ban any dramatized fights from your drama lessons, suggesting instead that any improvisations stop in the moment *before* the fight takes place. (This would, in fact, be a far more dramatically interesting place at which to stop – see the 'Clap fight' exercise below.)

Frog fight

- This is a great warm-up for when you are doing some work based on conflict.
- Divide the class into two. Create two lines down the centre of the room, with each person facing a partner.
- *Crouch on your haunches, with your hands raised in front of you, elbows bent, palms facing your partner at shoulder level.*
- *Now 'fight' your partner, but using your palms only, trying to over-balance the other person.*
- *You are not allowed to grab with your fingers and you must stay on your haunches to remain in the game.*
- *When one of you falls over, or stands up, the fight is finished. Relax while you watch the rest of the class competing.*
- When all the students have finished, the 'round' is over.
- The losing frog fighters stand to one side, and the remaining students again line up facing a new partner.
- This continues until there are only two people left. At this point, the final takes place and a winner is decided.

Clap fight

- Stand the class in a circle. Choose two volunteers to be the 'fighters'.
- The rest of the students begin clapping in a regular rhythm.
- As they clap, the fighters enter the circle and move around the space, sizing each other up.
- Gradually, the class should increase the speed and intensity of the clapping.
- The fighters respond to the increasing tension, getting ready to come to blows.
- At the point of highest tension, just before they strike each other, the improvisation stops.
- Talk afterwards about exactly what it was that created a feeling of tension.

Methods of conflict

- Divide the class into groups. This exercise works well with either pairs (just the two fighters) or small groups of about four (to include onlookers, referee, etc.).
- The students create freezes of different conflicts, one at a time.
- Give them a few minutes to discuss and create the freeze, then look at each group in turn.
- Your conflicts might include:
  o a Wild West style shoot-out
  o an historic duel
  o a championship boxing match
  o a sword fight
  o a playground brawl.

Riot!

- Work as a whole class. Alternatively this can be done with half the class at a time, with one half watching the other half perform and then swapping over.
- The students are protestors, police, etc. at a riot.
- They must create a series of freeze-frames in chronological order, like a series of flash photos taken by a photographer.
- They should start with the build-up to the riot, moving on through the riot itself, and then on to the aftermath.
- You might like to give them some time to discuss the exercise as a class before they begin, for instance deciding on different characters, what the protestors are protesting about, why the riot happens, etc. You could also pre-select five scenes, one for each of the freeze-frames.
- Alternatively, you might just go ahead without any planning and see what happens.
- Count down from ten to zero before saying 'freeze' for each image.

8

Advanced drama techniques

In this chapter, I look at a few more advanced drama techniques. You should be able to introduce these techniques with older students, and also with able younger children. In fact, the techniques described in this chapter can even be taught, at a basic level, to fairly young children. Children love being introduced to complex sounding technical terms and, as is often the case with technical terminology, many of them sound a lot more complex than they actually are. Your skill as a teacher will allow you to adapt the information you give to the age of your children.

I give ideas in this chapter for looking at subtext and character objectives, and also for exploring how dramatic irony works. There's also an introduction to the use of symbolism – the reading of 'signs' in a dramatic context. I make no claims, though, to be giving a comprehensive guide to all the different theatrical concepts. When looking at the advanced techniques described here, aim to develop your students' awareness of how they would impact on an audience. This will help them make judicious use of these approaches in their own drama.

Subtext

The term 'subtext' describes something that a character knows, which the audience and the other characters may (or may not) be able to guess or work out. The way that the actor portrays the character will be influenced by the subtext. In many cases, the subtext is quite a subtle thing that is never actually revealed, but which adds depth to the portrayal. Subtext can also add a great deal of dramatic tension to a situation.

For instance, imagine that a man is secretly in love with his brother's wife. He loves his brother, and consequently would never tell him his true feelings, for fear of damaging their relationship. However, his secret is hinted at in the way he becomes silent and moody whenever he is around the two of them. During the play it becomes obvious that, for some reason, he never wants to be left in a room alone with the wife. When this does happen on one occasion, he behaves in a particularly awkward way with her, so much so that she accuses him of hating her.

A great deal of dramatic tension can be added to a story by the subtext, as the example above demonstrates. Here are some exercises that you can use to show your children how subtext works.

What's my secret?

- Think of a range of different 'secrets' that characters might have. Make some slips of paper and write one secret on each one.
- With younger children you might use fairly straightforward secrets, such as:
  o you have a tummy ache
  o you are upset because your hamster is sick
  o you have some sweets in your pocket that you want to eat.
- With older students, you can include some more complex ideas:
  o you have won the lottery
  o you have a contagious disease
  o you fall in love with the first person who speaks to you.
- Divide the class into pairs or small groups.
- Now either:
  o give each student a slip with a secret on it
  o give only one student a slip with a secret.
- Tell them not to let anyone know what their secret is.

- Ask the groups to go straight into a simple improvisation, in which the characters know each other quite well. For instance, a scene in the playground or an office.
- At the end of the improvisation, the students should try to guess what the secrets were.
- Introduce the term 'subtext' to the class. Talk about how the secret in this scenario affected the characters' behaviour and how this might have an impact on the audience.

The tube train

- Place a line of chairs in front of the class. These are the seats on a tube train.
- About four volunteers enter the train in turn.
- Before each person enters, they are given a card with a 'secret' (i.e. subtext) on it, such as one of the following.
  o You can hear a loud ringing noise.
  o You hate confined spaces.
  o You think you know everyone.
  o You are a robber, scared of being recognised.
  o You are a plain clothes police officer.
- As the improvisation develops, and the characters interact, the rest of the class try to guess what the secrets are.
- If necessary, the tube train can get stuck in a tunnel. This will heighten the sense of tension.
- Encourage the students to be subtle about their secrets, rather than overplaying the subtext and making it too obvious.
- Afterwards, talk about how the subtext influenced characterization, and how it helped to add dramatic tension to the scene.
- You could do a similar improvisation set in a doctor's waiting room.

Objective and super-objective

Teachers will be very familiar with the term 'objective', in the context of what we want our students to achieve during a lesson. In drama, an objective works in exactly the same way, but instead it means what a character wants to achieve. The objective might be something that a person wants to achieve within a scene (a scene objective). It can also be something that a character wants to achieve during the play as a whole, which is known as a super-objective.

Putting an obstacle in the way of the character achieving his or her objective adds dramatic tension and suspense to a piece of drama. Indeed, many storylines are based entirely around a character wanting something but being prevented from attaining it.

What I really, really want

- Work in small groups.
- Give each person a slip of paper with an objective on it. Try to choose objectives that will conflict with each other. This will add plenty of tension and interest to the mix. For instance:
  o You want everyone to sit down.
  o You want everyone to stand up.
  o You want to get complete silence.
  o You want lots of noise and singing.
- The aim is to achieve this objective during the course of an improvisation.
- Give a simple scenario, for instance a family meal.
- Afterwards, talk about how each character's objective affected their behaviour, and the impact that this had on the scene and on the audience.

Dramatic irony

Dramatic irony describes a situation where the audience knows something that one or more of the characters do not. This leads to dramatic tension and can also be the source of a great deal of hilarity or, conversely, feelings of horror. This technique draws in the audience because we desperately want to tell the characters what is going on. Probably the best way to understand it is to give a couple of examples that you can use in the classroom.

Behind the sofa

- Place three chairs together to represent a sofa (or use a real sofa if you have one).
- Tell the students: *A parent comes into the living room. He or she drops something behind the sofa, and bends down (out of sight) to pick it up.*
- *Two young people return from a night out.*
- *They talk, in great detail, about all the things that they got up to at the party/in the club.*
- The audience is aware of the parent listening in; the children are not.
- *What effect does this have on us as an audience?*

Under the bed

- Place some blocks, chairs or tables to represent a bed. This needs to have a space under it.
- Tell the students: *the improvisation begins with a burglar entering through the bedroom window and looking around for things to steal.*
- *The burglar hears the occupants of the house coming up to the room, and hides under the bed.*
- This improvisation could then be taken in various different directions.
  - o For instance, the people settle into bed and turn off the light. Every time the burglar tries to leave, one or other of the couple gets up, drops a leg out of bed in his way, etc.
  - o Alternatively, the couple could begin discussing their secret stash of cash, cunningly hidden where no burglar could ever find it!
- Again, discuss the effect that the dramatic irony in this scene had on the audience.

Symbolism

A symbol is simply something that 'stands for' something else: for instance, the red light on a set of traffic lights 'stands for' stop. Our lives are full of symbols; they are so prevalent that we take it for granted that everyone knows what they mean. This can of course lead to some cross-cultural confusions. The activities below will help you explore symbolism and signs with your students.

Brands as symbols

- Today's children are very (perhaps scarily) familiar with the symbols connected to certain brands – McDonald's, Nike, Coca Cola.
- Because of this familiarity, brands offer a useful way into understanding symbolism for students of all ages.
- Talk with the class about how companies use their brands as a tool for recognition, but also as a symbol of what that product represents.
- Get hold of some images of different brands (you can do this through Google Image), or some branded items themselves.
- Show these to your children and ask what company each brand represents.
- Talk together about what these images might be 'saying' about the product or company.
- For instance, the Nike 'tick' has both positive connotations of being 'right', and is also a freeflowing image that suggests movement and sport.

The symbolism of colour

- Brainstorm the symbolism associated with different colours. For added interest, show your class a range of different coloured papers.
- If you have the resources available, it's a great idea to use different coloured lighting gels to show how colour can create a powerful sense of atmosphere.
- Begin with the colours that have obvious symbolic connections, such as red, blue, green and black.
- You might like to brainstorm as a whole class, or go round the circle with each student suggesting a word, image, emotion, idea, etc.

- Talk with the students about how they might link this colour to a piece of drama. For instance, with the colour red, we might imagine ourselves in:
  o an operating theatre or delivery room in a hospital
  o a seedy nightclub or casino
  o the scene of a murder
  o the middle of a *Reservoir Dogs*-style scenario.
- Divide the class into small groups and give each group a different colour to work with.
- If you have the time, you might ask that the students bring in props, costumes, etc. for a performance based around the symbolism of colour.

The symbolism of objects

- Props and objects can have a huge range of symbolic associations, and are often used to add extra levels of meaning to plays (and indeed to novels and paintings as well).
- Most religions use objects for their symbolic meanings, and there are many connections between different faiths in terms of their use of symbolism. For instance, light (candles, fireworks, etc.) features widely. Talk with your children about the symbolic objects they know of in different religions, and what they think these symbols might be 'saying'.
- Show your class a range of objects that might be thought to have symbolic connections, talking about the meanings they associate with each one. For instance, show a:
  o cross
  o candle
  o ring
  o sword
  o bowl of water.
- Divide the class into small groups, giving each group one of the objects. Ask the students to develop a scene that gives deeper levels of meaning to the prop.

For a really in-depth explanation of the whole area of semiotics (the reading of 'signs'), see www.aber.ac.uk/media/Documents/S4B/semiotic.html.

9

Themes for drama

This chapter gives four themes that can be used for drama in schools, with lots of ideas for activities within each one. Each theme is divided into a number of lessons, each of about an hour's duration. Hopefully, you will be able to adapt the ideas and approaches given here to use with other themes that you wish to cover. The first two themes are most suitable for younger students; the second two for older ones. Because of the restricted time that is typically available for primary drama, you could pick out a number of the simpler activities around one theme to cover in a single lesson. Secondary teachers should find plenty of useful material here for schemes across Key Stages Three and Four.

Communication

This scheme looks at the variety of ways in which we can communicate with other people. It also explores drama as a form of communication. After a short introduction to the topic, the class then works in role as a tribe of Native American Indians for a number of lessons. In my experience, the students become totally engrossed in the story of the tribe. They also love learning the sign language letters each week.

Lesson One: Let's communicate!

Whole-class discussion – Communication

- Talk as a whole class, sitting in a circle.
- Brainstorm all the different ways in which we can communicate with other people. This could include:
  o speech
  o sign language
  o body language
  o visual signals, e.g. smoke or torches
  o writing, including letters, emails, etc.
- Talk about the problems we might encounter when we're communicating, for instance being misunderstood.
- Introduce the idea of drama as a form of communication. *Who are we communicating with when we perform? What is the purpose of drama as a form of communication?*

Whole-class activity – Chinese whispers

- This classic game shows how communication can go wrong.
- Sit in a circle. Ask for a volunteer to start.
- The volunteer whispers a sentence or phrase to the person sitting next to him or her.
- *This phrase can only be said once each time – if you do not hear it, do the best you can.*
- It is then passed around the circle. The last person to hear it says it out loud to the class.
- *Has the phrase changed? Why has this happened?*

Paired activity – Move your partner

- *Work in pairs. Stand together in a space.*
- *Move your partner around the room, using only words.*
- *How easy or hard was this?*
- *Now move your partner around the room, using only gestures.*
- *Was this harder or easier, and why?*

Paired activity – Getting directions

- *Work in pairs. One of you is a visitor to a foreign country; the other is a native of that country. Neither of you speak the other person's language.*
- *The visitor needs to get directions to somewhere (the station, the bank, a hotel). He or she asks for the directions in English.*
- *The other student answers in a made-up foreign language.*
- *What ways do you use to make yourself understood when you do not speak a common language?*

Individual activity – Learning sign language

- Talk to the children about sign language, finding out what they already know about it.
- *Who might use sign language? Why do some people need to sign to communicate?*
- Explain that the students are going to be learning the British Sign Language alphabet.
- Depending on how long you have available for this scheme, teach the children about three to five letters per week, working your way through the alphabet.
- This could be done at the start or end of the lesson. Memorising the letters could also be set as a homework task.
- For more information, and images/animations of the sign language alphabet, see:
  o www.britishsignlanguage.com
  o www.british-sign.co.uk
  o www.dictionaryofsign.com.

Research task – Native American Indians

- Explain to the students that, for the next few sessions, you are going to be working in role as a tribe of Native American Indians.
- As a homework task, they should do some research into this subject, bringing in some ideas and information for the next lesson.

Lesson Two: The tribe

For this lesson you will need a 'speaking stick', which will be used during meetings. This should be an interesting-looking stick (or other object). If possible, make a decorative speaking stick by adding feathers, images, etc.

This lesson can proceed in several different ways. If you wish, you can control the story fairly tightly, by going in and out of role to set the various activities. Alternatively you could hand over the reins to the children fairly early on, allowing them to dictate the direction of the story.

Teacher in role – Welcoming the tribe

- Begin the lesson by going straight into role as the Chief of a tribe of Native Americans.
- Welcome the students in role and introduce the speaking stick, explaining that whoever holds the stick is entitled to speak without interruption.
- Establish a name for your tribe.
- Ask if anyone has any news to share with the tribe. Pass the speaking stick to any child who wishes to contribute.
- Sometimes, a really interesting suggestion will come up that you might like to follow up on, perhaps by going straight into an improvisation.
- Explain to the class, in role if possible, how you will call them to a meeting (for example, by banging the speaking stick against the floor).

Whole-class discussion – What were Native Americans like?

- At this point, you might wish to spend some time listening to feedback from the students about the research they have done.
- This can help younger children understand the kind of roles they are going to take on (see next page).
- With older students you might want to stay inside the story for all or most of this lesson.

Individual focus – My role in the tribe

- *Sit in a space on your own, eyes closed. Think about the kind of role you play in our tribe.*
- *Are you a warrior, a medicine man or woman, a child, a parent, a hunter?*
- *Think about the kind of character this person would be. Choose a name for yourself that reflects the role you are going to take on.*

Whole-class improvisation – Early morning in the camp

- *Now move into a frozen position that shows what you might be doing first thing in the morning.*
- *Perhaps you are preparing breakfast, sharpening spears, cleaning up your tent.*
- At a signal, unfreeze the class and ask the students to go straight into an improvisation.
- Some might continue to work alone, focusing on an individual activity. Others could begin to interact, for instance asking someone for help.

Whole-class meeting – The poisoned river

- Call the tribe to a meeting using the signal agreed earlier.
- Introduce the problem that they must solve. You could do this yourself, in role, or have a volunteer primed to put forward the problem, again in character.
- *The problem is that the river is poisoned, and that your [our] tribe must warn another tribe who live downriver. This tribe live a day's journey away, and speak a different language to your [our] own.*
- *Talk together about how you are going to warn them – what ways might you use to communicate?*
- Your children might suggest using smoke signals. Explain that the tribe are too far away to see them, and that you must travel, as a tribe, to warn them.
- Brainstorm the tasks that your tribe needs to complete before their journey.
- Bring up the issue of water if the students don't – how are

you going to find water to take with you, given that the river is poisoned?

Small group work – Preparing for the journey

- Give out the tasks, as agreed with the children.
- For instance, one group could prepare a map, another could collect food and supplies, another group could take down the tents, and another could go ahead to scout out the route.
- As appropriate, watch small group improvisations, display maps on the wall, etc.

Small group improvisation – Packing to go

- *In your groups, devise a short improvisation that shows you packing to go on the journey.*
- *Aim to put across your feelings and emotions about leaving this place, and also your fears and hopes about what lies ahead.*

Lesson Three: The journey

Whole-class meeting – Our journey

- Begin with a recap, in role, of the planned journey.
- What is the purpose of our journey?
- What kind of dangers and problems might we face on the way?

Small group freeze-frames – Danger!

- *In your small group, decide on a scenario where you face danger during the journey.*
- *For instance, you might be attacked by a wild animal, someone could get injured, you might run out of water*
- *Devise a set of three freeze-frames to show the beginning, middle and end of the scenario.*
- *Now work as a whole class to perform the freezes together.* Give three slow drum beats. On each beat, the children should move into the next freeze, in consecutive order.

Small group improvisation – On the journey

- Work in small groups to prepare an improvisation showing a scene from the journey.
- This might be a development of the freeze-frames, or it could be from a different point in the journey.
- Aim to include plenty of dramatic tension in your improvisation. You might like to talk with the class about the kind of things that are likely to create dramatic tension in the scene, for instance, an encounter with some wild animals or an injury to one of the group.
- Show some or all of the improvisations to the rest of the class, and talk about how dramatically interesting they are, and why this is.

Lesson Four: Communicating with the tribe

Whole-class meeting – How do we communicate?

- The tribe have reached their destination, and are about to try and tell the other tribe about the poisoned river.
- Talk, in role, about how you might do this. How can you overcome the language barrier and get your message across?

Whole-class improvisation – Passing on the message

- Divide the class in two. One half are going to play 'the other tribe', the rest will stay in the roles they have used so far.
- Depending on the age and experience of the children, you might go straight into a whole-class improvisation, or you might plan out the performance before you begin.

Small group performance – Celebration dance

- Once the message has been delivered, the two tribes decide to hold a celebration.
- Split the class into groups, and ask them to prepare a short celebration dance, showing what has happened during the course of the story.
- Get the groups to show each of the celebration dances in turn.

Whole-class meeting – Where to now?

- Hold a meeting, again in role, about what to do next. The tribe need to find a new place to live.
- *What kind of place are you looking for? What sort of considerations should you bear in mind? Would you like to join up with the other tribe or are you going to continue on your own?*
- If there is time, you could do some improvisations around setting up the new camp.

Bullying

Although schools are always finding new ways to deal with bullying, it is a perennial problem that seems to persist despite our best efforts. One really effective way to tackle the issue of bullying is through drama. Drama allows the students to empathize with the victims of bullying, by seeing what it would be like to be in their situation. It can also help them to understand why some people might become bullies, and what we can do to discourage them.

When looking at this theme, you will need to be sensitive to any issues that there might be within the class. Keep a close eye on the children's emotional reactions to the activities, taking note of anyone who seems concerned or upset. Let the students know that you are available if anyone wishes to talk to you in privacy about instances of bullying. Emphasize the positive aspects of building self-esteem, and ways of tackling bullying both at school and outside.

Lesson One: What is bullying?

Whole-class discussion – Bullying

- As an introduction, talk as a class about bullying.
- *What is bullying?*
- *What kinds of behaviour might be called bullying?*
- *Why do you think people bully others?*
- *What does it feel like to be bullied?*

Whole-class activity – Bully the chair

- Stand the whole class in a circle. Place a chair in the middle.
- The students take it in turns to come into the circle and 'bully' the chair.
- Afterwards, talk about the experience of doing this exercise. *How did it feel?*

Individual activity – Building self-esteem

- *Stand in a space on your own.*
- *Imagine you are very shy. Begin to walk around the space.*
- *Every time you pass someone, smile at them.*
- *Every time someone smiles at you, feel yourself growing slightly in confidence.*
- *As you become more confident, change the way that you walk, so that your movements become bigger and bigger.*

Paired activity – Compliments

- *Work in pairs. Try to go with someone you don't normally work with.*
- *Stand opposite each other and take it in turns to compliment each other.*
- *Gradually make your compliments nicer and nicer.*
- Afterwards, let the students talk about how it felt to take part in this activity.

Small group improvisation – Playground fun and games?

- *Working in small groups, prepare an improvisation in which a group of children are playing some games.*
- *A shy child approaches; instead of inviting the child to join in, the others begin to circle him or her, calling names.*
- *Aim to build up to a peak of tension then find some way to resolve the scene.*
- Watch some performances – what kinds of bullying are shown? How successful is each group at putting across the feelings caused by bullying?

Lesson Two: Bullying and emotions

Paired activity – Master/servant

- Do a few rounds of the master/servant exercise (see p. 52 for an explanation).
- Afterwards, talk about how it felt to be the servant. *How does it feel when someone bosses us around, and we feel that we have to do what they say?*
- *How does it feel to be the master? Is it always a good feeling to be in charge?*

Whole-class improvisation – What's your secret?

- In this exercise, the person who has the subtext does not know what his or her secret is.
- Ask for a volunteer – choose a student whom you know to be confident or send a pair of students together if you prefer. Send the volunteer(s) out of the room.
- With the class, choose a 'secret' that the person will have when he or she comes back in. For instance, they will have a weird haircut, be covered in green spots or have a black smudge on their nose.
- Get your volunteer to come back into the room. The whole class should improvise their reactions to the 'secret'.
- The volunteer should try and guess what the secret is.
- After the improvisation is finished, talk with the volunteer about how it felt to be singled out in this way.
- Run the improvisation again, giving other children the chance to see how it feels to be victimized.

Thought tracking – The first day

- One of the hardest times to feel confident and assertive is on the first day at school, whether at infant, junior or secondary level.
- *Sit in a space and close your eyes. Think back to how you felt on your first day at school. What were your worries and concerns? What kind of things made you nervous? What were your hopes for the future?*

- *Stand and take up a frozen position, showing your feelings through your body. Think of one thought that summarizes your emotions.*
- Move around the classroom. As you tap a student on the shoulder, he or she should say the thought out loud.

The thought alley – Victim and bully

- Set up a conscience alley or thought tunnel (see p. 26 for details).
- One side is going to be the bully's thoughts and feelings, the other those of the victim.
- Ask for a volunteer to walk down the middle. At the end, talk about how it felt to hear the two opposing kinds of emotions.
- Alternatively, all the students forming the alley could say the bully's thoughts first time round, and then the victim's.

Lesson Three – Bullying poem

Whole-class discussion – Recap

- Talk as a class about the issues and areas covered so far.
- Discuss how you might use some of the material and activities to develop a piece of drama.
- *Why might it be useful to develop an extended piece of drama around the topic of bullying?*
- *How could we use this drama to help others?*

Individual focus – The poem

- *Sit in a space with your eyes closed.*
- *Listen to the 'Bully' poem (see Appendix Three, pp. 188–9).*
- *What kind of emotions, ideas, feelings and thoughts does this poem bring into your mind?*
- *How might you use this poem as a starting point for a piece of drama?*

Small group performances – Using the poem

- Hand out copies of the poem to each group.
- *Talk together about your ideas for using the poem.*
- *Develop your ideas into a piece of drama.*
- *You might use the whole poem during your performance, use some extracts from it, or simply use it as a starting point or inspiration.*
- Watch the performances and talk about what each group has done with the text.

Lesson Four – Solutions to bullying

Whole-class discussion – Solutions

- Talk as a class about how we can deal with and perhaps solve the problem of bullying.
- *Who could you talk to if you were being bullied? What concerns do you have about telling someone, and how might these worries be overcome?*
- *What does the school do already to deal with bullying? What more might our school do in the future?*
- You might like to give your class the telephone number for ChildLine, in case any child needs to talk about the issues raised during this work, and does not wish to talk to someone at school. The free helpline number for ChildLine is 0800 1111.

Small group freeze-frames – Dealing with a bully

- *Working in small groups, prepare a freeze-frame to show one way of dealing with a bully.*
- *For instance, talking to a teacher, walking on by, getting a friend to support you.*
- Look at the freeze-frames and talk about the different solutions.

Small group improvisation – Adding solutions

- *Work in groups of four.*

- *Start with two bullies and one victim. Improvise a short scene.*
- *Now add another person, who should play a teacher. How might the teacher handle the situation?*
- *Now redo the scene, this time making your victim more assertive.*
- *What do we mean by being assertive? How can this help solve our problems?*

Small group performance/video – Stop the bully

- *You have been commissioned to devise a short video called 'Stop the Bully'.*
- *Work in your groups to decide what kind of things you might include.*
- If there is time, perhaps by extending this into the next lesson, it's a great idea to actually make the videos. If possible share the videos with the school, perhaps in a special assembly on bullying.

The Estate

This theme is probably particularly useful for teachers working in a city environment. For teenagers who actually live on an estate, or in an area where their friends or peers live on an estate, the following lessons will often have some very personal connections and resonances. For some of your students, their only 'experience' of estates will be via the often stereotyped versions taken from the television. It can be harder to achieve realism in these situations, but it is by no means impossible.

Once it gets going, you may find your estate takes on a life of its own. The following lessons should therefore be treated as guidelines/suggestions rather than as a blueprint. Be guided by where your students want to take the work.

Lesson One: Creating the Estate

Whole-class discussion – Starting points

- Begin with a whole class discussion about estates.

- Establish what your students' experiences are, and also any preconceptions they might have.
- Identify any estates in the local area.
- *What kind of people might live on these estates?*
- *What kind of issues, problems, challenges, etc. do you imagine the residents face?*

Whole-class warm up – Developing a group identity

- This warm-up focuses on developing a sense of group identity, in preparation for working as a community.
- *Stand in a circle, holding hands.*
- *Turn the whole circle inside out, without dropping hands.*
- *Now all stand at one end of the room.*
- *Move one person from one end of the room to the other – they must not touch the floor.*

Small group work – Setting up the flats

- Divide the class into small groups of about four to six people.
- If possible, aim for a good mix of personalities and genders in the groups.
- *First, decide on your characters and their relationships to each other.*
- *For instance, you might be a family, a group of students, a single parent with young children or a group of refugees.*
- *Using chairs, tables, and any other furniture that is available, set up your flat.*
- *Produce a freeze-frame to show who your characters are and what relationship they have to each other.*
- Look at each freeze frame as a class and interpret what is going on.

Whole-class work – Mapping the estate

- Bring the students back together as a class.
- Using a large piece of paper, work together to draw a map of the estate.

- Decide on a name for the estate, include the locations of the flats and other amenities.
- Talk as a class about the various locations on the estate – ask which ones might be useful for dramatic purposes, and why?

Individual writing – This is my life

- *Working on your own, write a short monologue about your life.*
- If there's time, some students could present their monologues to the class.
- Alternatively, the lines could be learnt for homework and performed in the next lesson.

Homework task – Possessions

- *Bring in one object to put in your flat.*
- *The object you choose should tell us something about your character.*

Lesson Two: Building relationships

Small group work – Building my character

- *Set up your flats and show your objects to the group.*
- *Each member of the group should talk about his or her object – what it means, how it relates to the character, etc.*
- *Read out your monologues to the group.*

Small group improvisation – Sunday morning

- *It's first thing in the morning on a Sunday.*
- *Develop an improvisation that shows what your characters are doing.*
- *Don't feel the need to do too much, or to create tension where there is none.*
- *Some of the characters might spend the whole improvisation asleep.*

- *After the improvisation, talk together about who might get on well together and where there might be tensions.*

Small group improvisation – Monday morning

- Repeat the exercise, this time improvising a typical Monday morning.
- *What differences are there between the two improvisations?*
- As a class, watch each group improvise one of their scenes. Talk about what is going on and how realistic the characters seem to be.

Lesson Three: Building a narrative

Whole-class brainstorm – Feelings and motivations

- *Sit in a circle.*
- *Going around the circle in turn, say 'I feel . . .' and then give one thing that you character feels.*
- *Now repeat with 'I am . . .'.*
- *Finally, repeat again with 'I want . . .'.*

Individual focus – Getting into character

- *Set up your flats in your groups.*
- *Sit in a space in the flat and close your eyes.*
- *Picture your character – think about your name, age, feelings, relationships, occupation, etc.*
- *Now picture the other characters in your flat – how do you feel about each of them?*

Paired improvisation – Gossip

- *Divide your groups into pairs.*
- *The first pair is in the living room of the flat, the others are out or in their rooms.*
- *In the pair, gossip or talk together about the other people in your flat.*

- *Swap over and repeat, so that everyone gets a go. You can mix and match the pairs as appropriate, or if you have an odd number of people.*

Small group improvisation – Building narratives

- Improvise some different scenes in your groups. Aim to build up dramatically interesting storylines.
- Use the following scenarios:
   o a happy occasion (this can go wrong towards the end if you like)
   o a sad occasion
   o a situation where a quarrel flares up
   o another scene of your choice.

Small group improvisation – Using a tight focus

- Now make it slightly harder for yourselves by using a tight focus.
- Repeat one of the scenes, but this time:
   o the first person to speak says two words
   o the second person says three words
   o the third person says four words
   o then start again from the beginning with two words.
- Now pick a different scene and try again, using a different focus.
- This time:
   o one person must be sitting
   o one person must be standing
   o one person must be lying down
   o one person must be strolling around
   o If you have more than four people, pick a specific posture for each one
   o As soon as a person changes position, someone else must take their place.

Lesson Four: Group interactions

Individual focus – My character

- *Close your eyes and reflect on the character you have built so far.*

- *What would make this person happy?*
- *What would make this person angry?*
- *Who are their closest friends and worst enemies on the estate?*

Paired improvisation – In the lift

- *Work in pairs, choosing a partner from another flat – preferably someone with whom your character has an issue.*
- *You both step into the same lift. It breaks down between floors.*
- *How do you react? Do you chat or stay silent? Do you get into a quarrel or fight?*

Whole-class tag improvisation – The visitors

- *In your groups, set up your flat.*
- *Freeze-frame in position in your houses.*
- *Choose one or two volunteers to start a tag improvisation.*
- *Your characters are going to visit one of the other flats.*
- *When you arrive at the flat, the people in that flat unfreeze and you should go straight into an improvisation.*
- *You might be visiting for a range of reasons. For instance, to:*
  - o *borrow some sugar*
  - o *ask for the return of some money*
  - o *invite them to a party*
  - o *ask them to turn down a noisy stereo*
  - o *complain about a barking dog.*
- Once the improvisation has finished, the visitors return to their flat and freeze-frame.
- At this point, one or two more students take over the improvisation.

Lesson Five: Objectives and status

Whole-class discussion – Creating conflict and tension

- Discuss the idea that a character + an objective + an obstacle will create conflict, i.e. that when someone wants something, and they are being prevented from having it, this provides a source of tension.

- Ask the different groups to identify the various conflicts in their flats and what is creating these.
- Talk about any groups that have a lack of dramatic tension in them, why this is and how it might be solved.
- Discuss the way that a character's objective can be linked to their status, i.e. they are more likely to get what they want if they are higher status (see the 'What's on TV' exercise below).

Small group freeze-frame – Showing status

- *In your groups, set up the flats.*
- *Create a freeze-frame to show the relative status of the characters in your flat.*
- Look at each group in turn, talking about how status is being shown.
- *Is it always the character who is literally 'highest' who has the highest status?*
- *How else can someone show or create status?*

Small group improvisation – What's on TV?

- *Improvise a scene in which your characters are watching TV. You are battling over who gets to choose the channel.*
- *At the start, one person is holding the remote control, but this can change during the scene.*
- *Perform the scene, in turn:*
  - *using numbers, counting upwards from one to about 50*
  - *using the alphabet, with each line starting with the next letter, i.e. the first line starts with 'a', the second with 'b', and so on*
  - *using words, but still retaining the strong body language and vocal expression from the previous two improvisations.*
- Watch some of the improvisations and talk about the varying levels of status and tension in each one.

Whole-class discussion – Status in a community

- Talk with the students about how some people have high or low status within the wider community.

146

- You might like to link this with the relative status that the students perceive within their own peer group.
- Discuss both the positive and negative qualities that can create status.
- *Who has the highest status on our estate and why?*

Whole-class tag improvisation – In the park

- Set the room up as a park or green area on the Estate, with a bench, swings, etc.
- A few of the characters enter the park one by one, establishing what they are doing there by how they move, what they do, how they interact, etc.
- There should be four people in the scene at all times.
- When one person leaves, this tags someone else to enter.
- An interesting variation is to freeze the scene, then ask the class to identify the person with the lowest status.
- This person must leave. To retain their place in the scene, the characters must establish their high status.
- Talk with the class about the idea of territory, and how this could be linked to status.

War

This theme is developed over several lessons or weeks, with the story moving on in a chronological order. The theme can throw up some emotional responses, and you should of course be sensitive to any students in your class who may have had personal experience of wars in other countries. If you do teach children with recent experience of wartime situations, it is probably best not to choose this theme for your class.

Your work might be based around study of the First or Second World Wars, or alternatively of a more recent conflict such as the wars in the Falklands, Afghanistan or Iraq. It is helpful for the students to have some background knowledge of the subject, so it might be wise to liaise with the History department to see which areas the students have covered. Alternatively, you might ask the students to do some background research before the topic commences, or set this research as homework tasks during the course of the lessons.

Lesson One: Leaving

Individual focus – Personal

- *Sit in a space with your eyes closed.*
- *Think about a time when you had to leave someone or somewhere, or when someone left you.*
- *Remember what happened in the situation. Why did you/they have to leave? What did you feel, physically/emotionally, and why?*
- *What are your strongest memories of that time, place or person? Try to bring back your sensory responses. What did you see, hear, smell, touch, taste?*

Individual focus – Character

- *Now imagine that you are about to leave the country to go to war.*
- *You are packing and taking a last look around your room. Recreate it in your mind.*
- *Use all your senses. What can you see, smell, hear, etc? Which items stir up your emotions? Why?*
- *Now stand up and get ready to pack. Move around your room, picking up items of importance and deciding what to pack. You only have a small suitcase.*
- *Take your time. Really try to visualize each of the items. As you pick them up, go through all the memories associated with them.*

Paired improvisation – The last morning

- *Decide what your relationship is, e.g. mother and son, brothers, etc.*
- *Now improvise a short scene which takes place on the morning you leave. You could be having breakfast, etc.*
- *Aim to create as much dramatic tension as you can, while still making the scene as realistic as possible. Remember the value of silence and*

stillness in building tension: there will probably be a lot of silent moments.

Paired improvisation – Saying goodbye

- *Now imagine you are at the train station, about to leave.*
- *Again, improvise the scene that takes place.*
- *This time try it with a different relationship, perhaps husband and wife.*
- *As you practice, think about how tension is created and sustained in this scene. How much speaking takes place? What sort of things are you saying?*

Freeze-frame – At the station

- Create a freeze-frame with the whole class at the station, in their pairs.
- Everyone should create a freeze-frame in the last few moments before the train arrives. (Some might be hugging, others crying, etc.)
- *Now take it in turns to unfreeze and improvise for a few moments.*
- *As one pair freezes, another starts.* (Use lights if you have them to indicate the changeovers.)
- *Can you control the improvisation as a whole class, allowing each pair to improvise and waiting your turn to unfreeze?*
- *This is difficult to do, but if it works it is very touching.*

Individual focus – On the train

- *Sit in a space on a chair on your own.*
- *Focus on your thoughts and feelings now that you are on the train.*
- *'Write' a diary entry about your day, saying what you are thinking out loud. Aim to focus only on what you are saying, rather than listening in to the others.*
- *Think about the emotions you have experienced in leaving.*
- *Talk too about your fears and hopes for the future.*

Lesson Two: Developing a character

Whole-class brainstorm – Arrival

- *Sit in a circle. Close your eyes and think about what a solider might feel on the day of arriving at an army camp.*
- *Now go around the circle, saying one word each in turn.*
- *Do not pause – if you cannot think of a word immediately, say 'pass' to keep the momentum going.*
- *Don't worry if you repeat something that someone else has said previously.*
- Go around the circle a few times, until the class have built up a picture of the soldier's arrival.
- *Now close your eyes again. This time think about what an officer might be feeling on the day that some new recruits arrive at his or her camp.*
- *Again, go around the circle saying one word each.*
- Afterwards, discuss the differences between the two 'types' of people.
- *How might an officer treat his or her soldiers? How would they feel about new recruits?*

Individual focus – On your character

- *Sit in a space on your own with your eyes closed.*
- *You are going to decide on a character for yourself.*
- *You could be an officer or an 'ordinary' soldier.*
- *Decide on your name, age, personality and background.*
- *Now focus on your feelings about being at the camp. Are you excited and keen or frightened and feeling sick?*
- *Try to avoid choosing a stereotyped character.*
- *However, do give yourself interesting personality traits.*
- *Remember that officers, as well as soldiers, may resent being in the war.*

Paired improvisation – Introductions

- *Stand up and open your eyes.*
- *If you have decided to be a solider, imagine you have just arrived at the camp.*

- *If you have chosen to be an officer, you are here to greet the new arrivals.*
- *Take up the 'stance' of your character, e.g. scared, in charge, etc.*
- *Go up to the nearest person and introduce yourself.*
- *Go straight into this improvisation, without asking your partner which type of character they are.*
- *Try to work out who they are by the way they are standing, the way they speak to you and what they say.*
- Afterwards, talk about how the students knew 'who' they were talking to, and how the differences in status were communicated.

Small group improvisation – The dugout

- *Work in groups of about four to six students, ensuring that there is a good mix of officers and soldiers.*
- *In your groups, set up an area as a 'dugout' or small camp, using tables, chairs, etc.*
- *Some of you have been here for a while, while others are new arrivals.*
- *Improvise a short scene on the day the new recruits arrive.*
- *How might the soldiers and officers who have been here a while react to the 'new recruits'?*
- *How will the status of the different characters affect who speaks/ takes charge?*

Small group planned improvisation – Tension begins

- *In your groups, discuss what minor tensions might arise between your characters.*
- *Chose one of these reasons and prepare a short planned improvisation*
- *What kind of things would cause tension?*
- *Remember, you are in a confined space and that can create conflicts.*
- *How would your character's feelings about the war affect the way this person behaves?*

Lesson Three: The tensions of war

Individual focus – On your character

- *Sit in a space with your eyes closed.*
- *Recap for yourself the character you created in the last lesson.*
- *Think about the other characters in your dugout group.*
- *Consider who you might like/dislike and why.*
- *Recap on your name, age, and personality, developing any areas that you left vague last time.*
- *Why are you here and how do you feel about it?*
- *Are there any other characters in your dugout with whom tensions might arise?*

Small group improvisation – Morning

- *Get back into your small groups and set up your dugout again.*
- *It is early morning and you are all asleep.*
- *Go straight into an improvisation.*
- *As you wake up, go about your morning routine, washing and preparing food, etc.*
- This improvisation will not contain a lot of tension.
- Afterwards, talk with the class about why the scene was lacking in tension. Establish how, if the improvisation is realistic, there may not be much talking or action going on.

Small group planned improvisation – Happy times

- *Plan and perform a short improvisation based on a 'happy' moment in your dugout.*
- *For instance, one of you receives news that your wife has had a baby.*
- *Again, discuss the scene afterwards.*
- *How much tension did this improvisation involve? Why was this? How did the different characters react to the 'good news'?*

Small group planned improvisation – Sad times

- *Now plan and perform a 'sad' moment in your dugout.*

- *For instance, you receive news that one of your friends was killed in last night's battle.*
- *How much tension is there here?*
- *Why is this different to the 'happy' improvisation?*
- *What might your characters be thinking/feeling?*
- *You might like to freeze during the improvisation and thought-track some of the characters' feelings.*

Small group improvisation – Waiting

- *While you are waiting for the call to battle, some more serious tensions arise.*
- Talk about why 'waiting' creates tension.
- *Decide between yourselves what is causing serious tension in your dugout.*
- *Go straight into an improvisation and see what happens.*
- *When you have finished, talk as a group about how the tension was shown. Was there lots of talking and action, or rather a sudden explosion after a long period of silence?*

Individual writing – A letter home

- *Write a letter home, telling your husband/wife, family member or friend what has been going on and how you are feeling.*
- *Talk also about your fears and hopes for the future.*
- *Consider how much information you would reveal to this person – would you keep quiet about certain aspects for fear of alarming them?*
- *Think carefully about how your character would view the events that have been going on.*
- *Are they looking forward to or dreading the moment the battle starts?*

Lesson Four: Battle!

Freeze-frame – The moment before

- *Set up your dug out.*
- *It is the moment before you go into your first battle. Freeze in position.*

- *What might your character be doing at such a stressful time?*
- *Remember, some people would react by being active, others by becoming introverted.*
- *Think about what would be going through your head – decide on one line that sums up your feelings.*

Whole-class discussion – Exploring the image

- Look at and discuss each group in turn.
- Identify the characters and the images they have created.
- *What are the characters doing? Why are they doing this?*
- Look closely at their body language in order to explore their emotions.
- Chose characters to say their 'line'.
- *Did we 'read' the body language correctly?*

Small group improvisation – Time to go

- *In groups, take up your frozen positions.*
- *Now go straight into an improvisation lasting one minute, which shows the scene just before the battle starts.*
- *This might be a very 'active' scene, but it might equally be quite still.*
- Discuss what creates the tension here and how it is shown.

Whole-class improvisation – The battle

- *It is halfway through the battle. Some of you are injured or dead, some alive.*
- Set up the whole space as the 'battlefield'. Split the class into two.
- *Half the class are going to improvise silently.*
- *The other half are going to create the sound effects – the soldiers' voices and other noises of battle.*
- *It is difficult to make this realistic. How much and what type of sound would there be?*
- Advise the students that they might chose to focus on one character and create 'their' sounds. *What would this person be saying?*

- Afterwards, discuss the improvisation. *How was tension most effectively created in this scene?*
- If there is time, swap the two groups over and repeat the exercise.

Small group improvisation – The aftermath

- *You are back in the dugout after the battle.*
- *Improvise the scene that takes place.*
- *Some of you might be tending to the injured and dead, others may well be in shock.*
- *This is effectively the 'resolution' of the tense battle scene.*
- *How much noise would there be now?*

Monologue – The impact

- *Sit in a space of your own in your dugout.*
- *In character, say the thoughts and emotions that are going through your mind in the aftermath of the battle.*
- *If you were 'killed' in the battle, you might chose to speak the thoughts of a loved one back home, perhaps on hearing the news of your death.*
- *What impact would the battle have had on the character you created?*
- *Would they be excited, stunned or terrified?*
- *How would the loved ones feel when they received the news?*
- This lesson can have a powerful impact. You might ask your students to write their thoughts up for homework.

Lesson Five: Prisoners of war

Individual focus – Captured

- *Sit in a space with your eyes closed.*
- *Imagine that you have been captured and that you are now a prisoner of war.*
- *You can keep the same character as you used in the last few lessons, or chose a different one.*
- *In your head, think about what your surroundings would be like. Where are you being held? What are the conditions here like?*

- *How is your character feeling about being captured? What are your fears about what will happen to you now? You may well be disorientated or injured.*

Individual monologue – Let me out!

- *Open your eyes and look around. It is dark, you are chained up and being held in solitary confinement.*
- *Each time you hear a drum beat, you become more and more frantic to get out.* (The teacher bangs a drum slowly, about ten times.)
- *You start to shout for help, getting louder and louder.*
- *You cannot move very far – how does that effect the way you are feeling?*
- *Try to let the panic rise gradually, from moving around to shouting for help in slow steps.*

Small group planned improvisation – Interrogation

- *Working in groups of three, place a chair in the middle of your space.*
- *One of you, the prisoner, sits in the chair.*
- *The others are the enemy and are going to question you about military secrets.*
- *You refuse to tell them what they want to know.*
- *Those students playing the enemy soldiers may, if you wish, use 'physical force' to compel the prisoner to talk.*
- Give the students ideas for potential interview and interrogation techniques that will create a sense of intimidation. For instance:
  o stand behind the person
  o lean in over a shoulder
  o stay still and silent
  o whisper in their ear
  o bang on the table
  o play 'good cop/bad cop' with a partner
  o prepare some nasty-looking equipment.
- Explore the best way of creating tension here – it is not necessarily through physical violence.

- The sense of threat should build slowly again, just as it did with the drumbeats previously.
- *How will the prisoner react as the tension rises? Will he or she crack eventually?*

Performance – Creating tension

- As a class, watch the group performances.
- Afterwards, discuss what happened, considering especially the creation of tension.
- How was tension created by the groups? Consider the body language, tone of voice, facial expressions, what the characters did, etc.

Large group improvisation – The minefield

- Divide the class into groups of about eight to ten people.
- The groups take it in turn to do the exercise, with the other students watching.
- Give out numbers randomly to each student, from zero to five. This can be done on paper or verbally.
- You should have about five zeros and then the numbers one to five.
- Ask the students to keep their numbers secret.
- The scenario is as follows: a group of prisoners of war are being forced to cross a minefield by their captors.
- The students should cross the length of the room to represent crossing the minefield.
- Before they begin, they should think carefully about how they would move, and what their body language would look like.
- As they move across the room, make five slow drumbeats.
- On the first drumbeat, the person with number one stands on a mine. On the second drum beat the person with number two is blown up, and so on up to five.
- The zeros do not step on a mine and make it across safely.
- Those who are not taking part should watch to see how tension is created.

- The tension in this situation is created by not knowing where the mines are, or who is going to get hit.
- *Is the tension higher for the audience or performers?*
- *What is your character thinking and feeling as you cross the minefield?*

Lesson Six: The innocent victims

Individual focus – The refugee

- *Sit in a space on your own with your eyes closed.*
- *Imagine that you are victim of war, a young refugee.*
- *Decide on your name, age, and which country you are from.*
- *Think about where your family are or what has happened to them.*
- *Decide also on the story of one incident that happened to you during the war.*
- *How would your character be feeling?*
- *Are they completely alone – without parents, brothers or sisters?*
- *Have they become separated from their family?*
- *Has their home been destroyed?*
- *How will the age of your character affect the way they think, feel and behave*
- *Can they speak any English?*

Focus and improvisation – Alone

- *Open your eyes.*
- *You are sitting in a refugee camp where you know no one else.*
- *Go straight into an improvisation.*
- *You may choose to sit still, on your own, or try to talk to somebody else.*
- *Your character may well be in shock and may not wish to move from where they are sitting.*
- *There may be language difficulties if you do try to communicate with someone else.*

Whole-class improvisation – The refugee camp

- Enter, in role, as the manager of the refugee camp.

- The following is a suggested outline for the improvisation. This could be adapted as required.
- The camp manager welcomes the refugees to the camp and introduces himself or herself.
- The manager asks the refugees to come and sit in a circle and introduce themselves, if they can.
- The manager then encourages the 'refugees' to tell their stories – who they are, and where they are from.
- Some of them may talk about what happened to them in the war.
- This improvisation could be developed in a number of ways, for instance with reunions of parents and children, re-enactments of scenes from the war, etc.
- If the students come out of character at first, they can be gently persuaded by you (the teacher in role) back into character.
- A friendly camp manager might encourage the refugees to share their stories.
- Alternatively, you could become an unsympathetic character who does not like refugees (perhaps have some sidekicks to help you).

10

Drama across the curriculum

It's my firm belief that drama can act as a fantastic medium for learning right across the curriculum subjects. In this chapter I'll look at how links to drama and the theatre might be made within the whole range of subjects. If you're a primary teacher, I'll show you how you could use drama techniques and activities to teach right across the curriculum. If you teach a subject at secondary level, and you'd like to make more use of drama in your lessons, then look in this chapter to find out how it can be done. Many of the ideas I offer have been kindly given to me by teachers that I've met in the course of my work.

Most of the suggestions below could be adapted to use with students of different ages, with just a few changes. For ease of reference, I deal with the curriculum subjects as they appear in the English National Curriculum, in alphabetical order (see www.nc.uk.net). I've omitted English, because of the clear links it already has with drama, and because guidance for teaching the subject is given with the English curriculum.

Art and design

There are many areas in which art and design are used within the theatre. I have regularly set tasks for a class that would be equally at home in an art lesson. Some of these are described below.

160

Mask making

- Work in pairs. Give each pair of students a balloon, which should be blown up to make the base for their masks.
- You will also need plenty of old newspaper and some water-based glue, mixed to a fairly wet consistency.
- Rip the newspaper up into small pieces, about an inch square.
- Wet the pieces of newspaper in the glue, and use these to cover the balloon.
- Smooth the paper down as you go, gradually building up the layers.
- You will need about four layers to make a firm base for your mask.
- Tie a short piece of string on each balloon and hang it up to dry.
- After about a week, the paper will be dry and the balloon will (usually) have deflated.
- Remove the balloon and carefully cut the balloon shape in half, to create two face-shaped pieces.
- These can then be decorated, and elastic attached.

Character collages

- Gather lots of old magazines, preferably those featuring plenty of photographs of people. Ask your students to help you get hold of these, perhaps as a homework task.
- Each student will need a piece of plain paper on which to create their collage and some glue.
- They should then go through the magazines, picking out various body parts, clothes, accessories, etc. to create a collage character.
- The characters could be created with several different objectives in mind. For instance, designing a costume or creating a monster character.

Citizenship

The council meeting

- Use the format of a meeting to encourage the students to explore a range of different perspectives. This activity will also

- encourage them to think about how the community can influence the choices made for a local area.
- Set up the room as for a meeting. Put a line of chairs at the front where the panel will sit, then rows of chairs facing for the 'locals'.
- Introduce the scenario by showing the students a letter. This letter explains how the school is planning to sell off part of the sports field to a supermarket.
- Stage a council meeting at which local people are asked to give their thoughts, ideas and comments.
- Choose volunteers to play the people sitting on the panel – this could include councillors, the head teacher, and supermarket representatives.
- The panelists explain the proposal and why they think it would benefit the community.
- Ask the students to think of a character, then join in the discussion, raising issues and asking questions in role.
  - o For instance, this might include parents and children who oppose the idea, local people who need work and who support it, environmental campaigners, and so on.
- As the meeting draws to a close, you might like to hold a vote to establish the consensus of opinion.

Design and technology

Stage sets

- Get hold of lots of differently sized boxes, made of fairly sturdy cardboard.
- Remove one side wall of the box to create a 'stage'.
- Give the class a design 'brief', specifying the play for which the set is going to be used, the type of atmosphere you wish to be created, a specific genre within which to work, etc.
- Alternatively, you might get the students to choose and research a play of their own.
- Give the students lots of junk modelling materials, wallpapers, paints, etc. with which to design and build a stage set.

- If applicable, your stage sets might be linked to a school production that is going to take place.
- If you take this route, you might hold a competition, displaying the finished stage sets and asking the rest of the school to judge which stage set should be used.
- The class could then be involved in the construction of a full-scale set taken from one of the designs.

Geography

Flights of fancy

- This activity is great to use when you are studying a country, say India, and wish to add some atmosphere, interest and imagination to the topic.
- Set up your classroom as an aeroplane. Create blocks of seats, two or three across, all facing in the same direction.
- Meet the students at the classroom door and invite them to get onto the plane for their flight to India.
- If you have the time and inclination, make some tickets for the flight to hand to the students.
- If you plan to use this approach several times over for different countries, you might get them to create their own 'passports', which can then be stamped with a visa for each country you 'visit'.
- Once all the passengers are seated, come to the front of the plane and give the class a flight safety demonstration, doing your best air steward impression.
- Tell the students that today they are flying to India, that they will be cruising at 28,000 feet, that there are six emergency exits on the aircraft, and so on.
- Now you are ready to take off. As the plane lifts into the air, get the students to tilt back their seats and make some engine noises.
- If you're feeling generous, you might give everyone a drink and snack during the 'flight'!
- For some fun, the plane could hit turbulence on the way to India.

- As you land, and the passengers disembark, have lots of engaging resources to welcome them to the new country. You might include:
  - exotic fruits, such as pineapples and coconuts
  - a range of spices used in Indian food – cumin, turmeric
  - several examples of sari fabric
  - some Indian music playing in the background
  - an extract from a Bollywood film playing on your interactive whiteboard.
- At this point, the lesson could go in a range of different directions, from some in-role writing about the sights and sounds of India, to looking at maps and locating different major cities, and so on.

History

There are many connections between history and drama: both subjects look at how different people behave in different situations; and in both there is interest in why people do certain things and the kind of conditions that might make us behave in a particular way. Clearly, history deals with the factual whereas drama deals with the imaginative. However, one of the key concepts that history teaches us is that the interpretation of events will vary according to the perspective from which a person views the situation.

Eyewitness account

- This is a fun activity with a dramatic opening that is sure to grab your class's attention.
- It also helps make an important historical point – that eyewitness accounts cannot necessarily be trusted.
- You will need to arrange for a helper – perhaps a member of staff who is free and willing to help, or in a secondary school, a sixth-form student. This person should preferably be someone that the students will not know terribly well.
- The teacher begins the lesson by telling the class that they will be looking at the reliability of eyewitness accounts.

- In the middle of the teacher's explanation, the helper bursts into the room, runs across to where the teacher is standing and slaps him or her in the face (use a pretend slap, obviously – it's worth doing a quick practice beforehand).
- The helper then runs straight out of the room.
- The teacher challenges the class: 'You have three minutes to write an eyewitness account of what just happened. Write down everything you observed, from what the person looked like to the colour of his or her clothes.'
- When the accounts are written, brainstorm with the class to see how much (often differing) information you can gather. Draw up a 'photofit' of your attacker on the board.
- When the photofit is complete, ask your helper to return to the room. Compare the real person with what the students remembered.

Historic recreation

- Recreate a setting from a particular time period in your classroom – for instance, a medieval village.
- Look at the different aspects of life at this time, for instance the food, the medicine, the entertainment. As far as possible, aim to recreate the experience as it would have been, as fully as you can.
- For this purpose, you might use make-up (the plague), scenery such as straw, rough materials for clothing, types of food in this period of history, and so on.

ICT

The school production

- There are many opportunities in ICT lessons for supporting a school show.
- For instance, the students could:
  - design posters to publicise the show
  - create some set designs using drawing software
  - write and design a programme for the show

165

o design some costumes
o add a page to the school website to help promote the production.

Mathematics

The teddy bear's picnic

- This is a great imaginative activity for introducing the concept of division to young children.
- Ask each child to bring in a favourite teddy or other cuddly toy.
- You will need to get hold of a large picnic blanket or rug, and also some food and equipment for holding a picnic.
- If it's nice weather, you might do this activity outside.
- Explain to the children that you are going to hold a teddy bear's picnic.
- Each teddy needs to have a fair share of the food.
- Show the children different foods – sweets, fruit, pizza, cakes. Talk about how they could divide the food up equally between the teddies.
- Share out the food and enjoy!

Modern foreign languages

The market

- Work as a whole class to create and set up a market that is held in the relevant country.
- Brainstorm the kinds of words and phrases that would be used in a market. These could be learnt for a homework task. The students could then work in pairs to practise various exchanges that might take place in the market.
- On the day of the market, set up your classroom or other space with stalls.
- Where possible, use real-life resources, such as money, food, and other products that are sold at the market.

- If you can spare the time, it's a great idea to run the lesson over into a break or lunch time, and invite other students to visit your market.

Catwalk

- The class work together to design, create and perform a catwalk fashion show.
- Again, lots of preparation time will be needed in the lessons running up to the event.
- Delegate various jobs, according to the students' individual preferences. For instance, you will need:
  o designers to make or gather the clothes
  o producers to stage the show – creating the runway, choosing music, adding any special effects
  o models
  o a presenter.
- Spend several sessions preparing – the students will need to look up and learn vocabulary, gather the outfits, plan the show, and so on.
- Stage your catwalk show, if possible inviting guests from other classes.
- Afterwards, the students could write up a newspaper report about the event.

Music

The panel

- Set up the room in the format of a chat/panel show, with a row of chairs at the front for the panel and the rest of the audience facing them.
- Ask for volunteers to play musicians both from the past and from the present day.
- Spend some time researching the kind of musical ideas these musicians have.
- Get the rest of the class questioning the musicians, in role, on the kind of music they create.

- They could also talk with the panel about which kinds of music they like and why.

PE

Keeping it safe

- Choose a volunteer to play a character who dresses inappropriately for sport.
- Before the lesson, dress this person in a way that is likely to be dangerous, for instance with jewellery, badly fitting trainers, clothes that might get caught in apparatus, etc.
- Put this person in the 'judgement chair' (see p. 24). Ask the rest of the class to pass judgement in turn about how and why this person needs to 'keep it safe'.

Science

The scene of the crime

- Set up a crime scene in your room or lab, with lots of props, pieces of evidence, items to be checked with forensics, and so on.
- Add a 'body', either by chalking or taping on the floor, putting a cloth with some body-shaped padding underneath, or by 'borrowing' a teaching assistant, sixth-form student, or other willing victim.
- If possible, get some crime scene tape, gloves, fingerprint powder, etc. to add realism.
- When the class arrives, tell them there has been a murder. They must act as detectives to solve the crime.
- Talk together about the various kinds of evidence that might be left at a crime scene – this will include biological, physical, chemical and other types.
- Choose a 'chief of police' to wear the gloves and hold up the various bits of evidence. Talk with the class about what kind of tests they wish to perform.

- Split the class up into groups and ask them to devise a theory about what has happened.
- Useful websites to get hold of resources for this lesson include:
  o www.uktapes.com
  o www.k9sceneofcrime.co.uk
  o www.johnadams.co.uk/detective_kit.html
  o www.curiousminds.co.uk

Religious education

Thought tunnel – how did it feel?

- Choose a point in a religious story where a person faces a challenge or problem, or where the person faces some difficult emotions.
- For instance, Jesus or Judas on the night before Jesus was crucified.
- Set up the thought tunnel in an open space (see p. 26 for more details on doing this).
- Ask the students in the two lines to say the thoughts or feelings of the character, as the person walks down the tunnel.
- Afterwards, feed back as a class on the experience.

Careers education

Careers in action

- This activity would work well at a whole-school options or careers day.
- Set up several rooms or areas as though they were locations where different jobs would take place.
- For instance, you might have a hairdressing salon, a building site, an office, a supermarket, a dentist, a hospital, and a vet's practice.
- Where you can, get in professionals (parents, volunteers from the local community), to help, advise and if possible to loan you some equipment.

- The more props, uniforms and 'real life' items you can add, the better.
- The students can then try their hand at various careers, getting a sense of the reality of what a particular job is like.

PSHE

Just say no!

- Brainstorm as a class all the pressures that young people might have put on them to do things that they know they shouldn't.
- Your list might include bullying, drugs and drink, stealing, and truanting.
- Split the class into pairs. Give a topic: one student must try and persuade the other to join in with something wrong or illegal.
- The other student should find a range of ways to say 'no', if possible giving reasons for turning their partner down.
- Swap over the roles and then watch some pairs doing their improvisations.

11

Staging a successful school production

In this chapter you'll find ideas, information and advice about staging a school production. School shows range from the classic primary school Christmas play devised by the class teachers, to the large-scale secondary production involving hundreds of students and staff. The advice given here will help you choose and mount a successful and enjoyable school production.

Choosing a production

Choosing the right kind of show can make the difference between a successful school production and one that goes down like a lead balloon. The following lists of pointers and questions should all help you make the right choice of production.

Appeal

- What is going to appeal, not only to your students but also to the potential audience of parents, friends and others?
- You also need to choose something that you're actually going to enjoy staging. After all, you're going to be putting a lot of your own free time into this.
- Don't forget to check with the relevant managers before choosing a show – they might have reservations about certain 'types' of play. This is obviously important if you wish to stage a play

with challenging content or language. If you get the support of senior managers ahead of time, this will help you defend yourself against any parental questions or complaints.

Type of production

- Do you plan to stage a musical, a straight play or a comedy?
- Would it be best to put on a well-known show that everyone will know?
- Alternatively, would you like to devise something new with the help of staff and students?
- There are also plenty of people willing to offer you plays and musicals for sale over the internet. Although these may be great, do consider whether you would be better off opting for a show that people will have heard of.
- If you are tempted to choose a difficult or 'challenging' play, be aware that this can put off potential members of the audience.

Cost

- Before you begin, make sure you know exactly what your budget is, and what it is going to have to cover.
- Perhaps you don't have a budget at all, in which case are you planning to ask for help from parents to organize and buy costumes, props, etc?
- Are you expected to meet all the costs through ticket sales?
- Alternatively, is your school willing to bear part of the cost in return for the considerable kudos that a successful production can bring? It's always worth asking for some kind of contribution from the school.
- How much will it cost you to stage the production, including the cost of the relevant licence for the performances?
- A fellow member of staff with expertise in devising spreadsheets is an asset in helping to prepare a proper budget.

Practicalities

- When making your final choice of show, be sure to think through all the practicalities of rehearsing and staging it.

- With a long or complex play, are you going to have enough time to rehearse the whole thing?
- If there are lots of lines, are you sure that your students are going to be able to learn these?
- Check on the number of parts actually available in the play, and how much onus is going to be on a relatively small number of actors.
- It's always useful to have lots of small parts to give out to students who just want to take part in some way. This also helps ensure that there are plenty of parents in your audience.
- Consider the size and potential of your stage and auditorium. Thinking about the technical aspects such as sets, lighting, etc., is it going to be possible for you to stage this play?

Casting

Casting can be great fun for those involved, but it does need to be handled with sensitivity. The following advice should help you pick the right cast, and also deal with the inevitable tears from those who are not chosen.

- I've found it works well to hold a short drama lesson to assess the overall ability of the students. During this session you can also check on their ability to cooperate and work as a team.
- You might also ask individuals to present a brief group improvisation and, in addition, to memorise a short scripted piece to check that they are able to learn lines.
- If you have a large number of people auditioning, split the auditions over several days rather than trying to do them all at once.
- Once you've narrowed down the list of students and decided who might take a main role, use a second round of auditions to assess them further.
- Think about how and when you are going to audition, and how you will divide up the time. Are you going to hold auditions after school or in break times? How much time will you need for group activities and then individual assessments?

- When casting for television, films, etc. the 'look' of an actor is all important. This is much less important for a school production, although obviously it still plays an element in your decision.
- Bear in mind the need for a wide range of students to get involved. Try not to typecast anyone into particular roles just because of their 'look'.
- Consider giving chances to the less academically able children, or those who are not generally regarded as trustworthy. Sometimes, the chance to appear and succeed in a school production can act as a turning point in their school careers.
- Make sure you cast some understudies or stand-ins for the bigger roles. Some students might drop out during rehearsals, others will fall sick on the night of the show. If at all possible, allow your main understudies a chance to perform, for instance on the middle night of a three-night run.

Budgeting

Depending on the size of your production, budgeting might be a reasonably straightforward job, or a mammoth task. The tips, thoughts and questions below should hopefully help you with preparing a budget.

First, work out the overall amount of your budget. Within this figure, you might include:

- money given to you by the school in order to stage the show
- potential revenue from ticket sales (total number of seats × price per ticket)
  o Think carefully about how much you want to charge the audience – it is best to keep the price as low as you can, in order to get a full house. It may not be possible or appropriate to actually charge your audience, and you will have to find other sources of revenue
- any other money, for instance from events held to support the show, sponsorship deals with local businesses, etc. (see also 'revenue sources' opposite).

Now work out how you are going to spend your budget. The following points should help you do this.

- Consider which parts of the production need what in terms of finance. If you are planning on having complex lighting, now is the time to get an approximate figure, as this can be costly.
- Look at the various production team jobs listed below. Talk with the individuals in charge of each area, asking them to prepare a brief outline of what they think they might need to spend.
- Work out how much you are going to have to spend on a licence for the production.
- It's always a good idea to have a contingency fund – there are bound to be unforeseen problems that will require money to solve.
- Set some money aside for photocopying and other administrative details.

Revenue sources

As well as getting money from your school, and from a paying audience, there are various other potential sources of revenue. You might make money from:

- photographs and videos of the show (make sure that you get parental consent from cast members before doing this)
- sales of food and drink on the night or nights of the show
- programme sales
- sales of other merchandise, for instance you might get some t-shirts made up and sell these to cast, crew and other interested parties
- in some schools, the PTA will be willing to allocate some funding to help put on a really great show.

The production team

Depending on the size of your school and the scale of your production, you might be working with a team of ten or more volunteers, or perhaps just with a couple of other teachers. I've outlined the main roles below, explaining the kind of jobs that each person might do and giving some tips to how you can keep things running smoothly. Clearly, there will be give and take as and when necessary between the various members of the team, and there may be a crossover between some of the different roles. There might also be the need for one person to take on two or more of these jobs.

Producer

The producer is responsible for organizing the staging of the production, and is in charge of pretty much everything apart from the actual direction of the play. The producer might arrange a license for the play, organize and keep a handle on the budget, make sure everyone in the production team completes their jobs on time, etc.

Director

The director is responsible for choosing, casting, rehearsing and staging the play. He or she will make the overall artistic decisions about all aspects of the production.

Musical director

If you are staging a musical, you will need to work in close conjunction with a musical director, often the head of the music department. The musical director will be in charge of casting, rehearsing and often conducting the musical aspects of the performance – both for the singers and for the musicians.

If you are not a musician yourself, if can be hard to understand just how difficult it can be to get the music side of a production organized. Ensure that you get any musical scores and tapes to your musical director as early as possible. When planning your final rehearsals, make sure you leave lots of time for any orchestra to set up, to rehearse songs, check sound levels, and so on. If possible, if can be useful to have a separate musical dress rehearsal, before you put the music and the acting together.

Set designer

The set designer's job is to design and create any sets, furniture, and other large items for the show. Often, this job falls to someone from the art or design and technology departments. Typically, he or she will rope in a team of students to help out with painting, or might incorporate the work into some lessons.

Stage manager

The stage manager is in charge of managing everything that happens on stage on the night of the show. He or she will be backstage on the night, directing the stage crew and making sure that the cues, set changes, curtains, etc. all happen correctly. Depending on how you allocate the jobs, the stage manager might also be responsible for dealing with any special effects (alternatively, this job might go to the lighting or sound crews).

Stage crew

For plays with lots of set changes, the stage manager will need a team of helpers, typically made up of older students. These students are responsible for set changes, opening and closing curtains, ensuring that props are handed out and returned, etc.

Props manager

The person in charge of props is responsible for getting hold of them, whether buying them, borrowing them or arranging for them to be created. On the night(s) of the performance, the props manager will help ensure that the props are on stage at the relevant point. This might mean setting them up beforehand, or giving them to the actors as and when required.

For a longer production with several scenes and a number of props, it can be useful to set up a series of tables in chronological order, from which the props can be taken. For a show that runs over a series of nights, it is obviously vital to ensure that props are returned and checked before the next performance.

Costume design and production

You will probably need a few people to help you out with the design and production of costumes, as this can be a complicated area. Parents are often more than happy to help out with getting hold of costumes. The costume design team might also need to hire any more complicated costumes, and there are plenty of theatrical suppliers who might be willing to do you a deal. During the run-up to the show, ensure that costumes are kept organized, clean and tidy. Ask that each cast member bring in a hanger, labelled with his or her name and role. If possible, get hold of some free-standing rails where you can store the costumes in a set order.

Publicity team – sales and marketing

The publicity team is responsible for marketing and selling the show, coming up with good ideas in conjunction with the producer or director, and putting them into action. The sales and marketing team might also help out with ticket sales. This is a great job to hand over to any business students, or perhaps to some sixth formers with an interest in enterprise.

Lighting team

The lighting team are responsible for ordering, setting up and operating the lighting for the show. Leave plenty of time before and at the technical rehearsal (see 'Technical rehearsal' p. 182) for them to set up and position the lights.

Sound production

The sound production crew will work on any aspects to do with sound in the show. This might include getting hold of microphones, setting up speakers, finding sound effects and checking sound levels.

Prompter

The prompter 'gives' a line to an actor who has forgotten what to say. It's best to choose an adult for this job, as it's harder than it might seem to both follow the play and also to know when to jump in and when to keep quiet.

Front of house

The front of house team will be responsible for ticket sales, collecting tickets on the night of the show, showing the audience to their seats, organizing and selling refreshments and programmes, and so on. Typically, you can rope in older students and parent volunteers to help with this job.

The audience

It's easy to get sucked into the fun, excitement and mayhem of rehearsing your show, and to forget about the audience that you hope to wow with your production. It really is worth thinking ahead of time about how you are going to get a full house, and what your audience will be expecting from the school show.

Getting an audience

Sometimes getting an audience is easy. Let's say your Christmas play is on for one night only, it's staged in a small school hall, and it involves every child attending your primary school. In these circumstances, you will have a ready-made audience of parents, friends and family who can hardly wait to come and see it.

However, if you are staging a large show over several nights, and one which only involves a relatively small cast, you will need to work harder to find an audience. If you've spent a small fortune on mounting the production, paid a fee for the licence, and have the headteacher breathing down your neck, then getting a paying audience in is vital.

- Be realistic about who is likely to make up the majority of the audience – it will probably be mostly parents, family and friends of the students. Focus on selling to these people, making sure that everyone who *might* want to come actually does.
- Don't make ticket prices outrageously expensive. Although selling fewer tickets at a higher price might make sense financially, this can alienate your potential audience and mean that your cast are performing to a handful of wealthy parents. Better to have a full house every night than to charge high prices.
- Ask each member of your cast and crew to sell a set number of tickets each. This will guarantee you at least a reasonable-sized audience.
- Publicize the production in school assemblies, perhaps performing a short scene or a song to the rest of the school.
- Have a stall with ticket sales in a prominent place during breaks and lunchtimes. Start selling tickets early on and throw in the odd comment about how they are 'selling like hot cakes'.
- Ask form tutors (in the secondary school) or class teachers (at primary level) to help you publicize the show at registration times.
- Set up some competitions and other promotions, to increase the word of mouth and the 'buzz' around the production.
- Design your posters early on, making sure that they are colourful and eyecatching (the classic 'Don't come and see this show unless . .' often works well).
- Stick posters up everywhere you can think of: around the school, in local shops, in the windows of students' houses.
- If there are any school events before the show (for instance, an open evening or a PTA barbecue), then ask if you can have a sales team there.
- Consider using some 'guerilla marketing' techniques, for instance stickers around the school with key quotes from the show, to get a 'buzz' going about the event.
- Get in touch with your local papers and radio stations and encourage them to publicize the event.
- Give free tickets to journalists in the hope of receiving a good write-up, and make sure that you have some high quality

photographs available. This won't necessarily bring in money this time round, but it's good publicity for the school.

- Get some free publicity via your school website.

Rehearsals

How long you have for rehearsals will very much depend on your individual situation. The following advice is based on (sometimes bitter) experience of the whole rehearsal process.

- As one of your very first jobs, create a rehearsal schedule that gives allocated time slots for rehearsing different parts of the show.
- If appropriate, it's best to rehearse the production in chronological order, although sometimes it is worth getting a group of characters who appear only in a few specific scenes to run through these scenes back to back.
- It's also worth rehearsing a scene involving the entire cast early on. This gives you the chance to talk with everyone about how you expect them to approach rehearsals. It also allows you to start building that essential sense of camaraderie and teamwork.
- Make it clear to your cast that missing rehearsals is a cardinal sin. There are few things more frustrating than not being able to rehearse because a couple of people are missing.
- Where students miss two or more rehearsals without an excellent reason, it is probably best to sack them early on and find someone else to fill the role.
- Leave more time than you think you will need for rehearsals. It is always better to have a few extra days rather than run out of time.
- Incorporate some warm-up activities at the beginning of each rehearsal. This helps loosen everyone up and get them in the right frame of mind.
- Make sure you say 'thank you' to your students for giving up their free time.
- Have fun, but also have an ethic of discipline, professionalism and hard work.

181

Technical rehearsal

The technical rehearsal, or 'tech', does exactly what it says on the tin. It is used for organizing all the aspects of the production that don't involve the performance. Things such as changing sets, checking lighting positions and cues, and organizing prop collection will all be rehearsed at the 'tech'. The actors simply 'block' their moves, standing in the relevant position at the right moment. The main people involved will be the stage crew, lighting crew, sound team and props team.

Dress rehearsal

Run a tight ship at your dress rehearsal. If possible, schedule it during the school day, so that everyone is fresh and ready to work. Depending on circumstances, this might also allow you to invite a small audience of other students to give the cast a reality check about performing in front of an audience. If it is not possible for you to take up school time, you will need to warn the cast well ahead of time that there is going to be a weekend dress rehearsal. With shorter plays, it may be possible to run the dress rehearsal in the afternoon or evening, directly after school.

Make the timings of the day clear to everyone, and insist on punctuality. When the dress rehearsal begins, it should to all intents and purposes run exactly like a real performance. Insist that the cast keeps going rather than stopping if anything goes wrong. They will need to do this 'on the night'. Don't worry hugely if your dress rehearsal goes horribly wrong. There's a bit of a theory in the theatre that an awful dress rehearsal means a great first night. Hopefully this will prove to be true for you!

Top tips for a successful performance

Somehow, I've managed to survive the trauma and excitement of countless school productions, both small and large scale. The following tips, gleaned from my experiences, should ensure that your performance runs as smoothly as possible.

- *Limit access to side stage*: The sides of the stage can be a busy place during the actual performance. The temptation to peek out and wave to mum or dad can be almost overwhelming for many children. It's best to ensure that only those people actually needed at any particular moment are actually side stage. Otherwise, things tend to become very chaotic and begin to look unprofessional.
- *Keep your cast tucked away*: The actors will be full of adrenalin and do tend to get overexcited. If at all possible, keep the students safely tucked away in a classroom nearby. Employ a very reliable set of runners to fetch the cast as and when they are needed. You could allow the main characters to remain side stage, as they are likely to be onstage for all or most of the time.
- *Encourage a professional approach*: Even with the youngest students, it pays to demand a high level of professionalism. Ask that your actors stay backstage the entire length of the play, rather than coming out in costume to meet and greet parents and friends.
- *Get someone to organize presents/flowers/cards*: Make sure you delegate the job of buying presents to thank the various members of your team. Hopefully, someone will remember to get something for you! Try not to make endless speeches on the last night – let the performance itself do the talking.
- *Manage the aftermath*: Consider who is going to help you tidy up after the event. The stage crew should play a part in this, and if you also involve the whole cast, it can turn into a fun winddown rather than a drudge.

Appendix One: Vocabulary list for drama

The list of words below should prove useful to you and your students in talking about and writing about drama. Younger students might learn the spellings or look up definitions of these words in a dictionary. Older students would be expected to use all these terms and more in writing essays and other pieces during their drama studies.

actor	freeze-frame	script
audience	group	status
blocking	hot seat	subtext
body language	imagination	symbolic
character	improvisation	visualize
characterisation	improvise	voice
communication	lighting	
concentration	mask	
conflict	mime	
cooperation	monologue	
costume	perform	
creativity	performance	
dialogue	props	
drama	realistic	
dramatic irony	relationship	
dramatic tension	role	
facial expression	scenario	
focus	scene	

Appendix Two: Internet links for drama

www.nationaldrama.co.uk – The website of the subject association for drama teachers.

www.stagework.org.uk – A very useful site set up by the National Theatre and some of its regional partners. You can find some great lesson plans and resources on this site.

www.nationaltheatre.org.uk – The website of the National Theatre.

www.shakespeares-globe.org – The website of the Globe Theatre in London.

www.artsonthemove.co.uk/education/education.html – This company offers drama training and workshops. Their site has some useful articles on both primary and secondary school drama.

www.universalteacher.org.uk/drama/drama.htm – This link includes some useful ideas for drama lessons. It's aimed at teachers in secondary schools, but might prove useful for primary school teachers as well.

Appendix Three: Texts for drama

You might like to use the texts given in this section as an inspiration for some drama work. Ideas for using the extract from *Macbeth* are given on pp. 79–80. The 'Bully' poem could be used to link in with the themed work given in Chapter 9, or perhaps for part of some PSHE-related lessons. The script 'Can you Keep a Secret?' might prove useful for work on developing dramatic tension, and also as a way of looking at the connections between actor and audience. Please note, although the second two texts are copyrighted, you are welcome to photocopy them as required to use with your class or classes.

Macbeth, Act 1, Scene 1

Thunder and lightning. Enter three witches.

First witch:
When shall we three meet again
In thunder, lightning, or in rain?

Second witch:
When the hurlyburly's done,
When the battle's lost and won.

Third witch:
That will be ere the set of sun.

First witch:
Where the place?

Second witch:
Upon the heath.

Third witch:
There to meet with Macbeth.

First witch:
I come, Graymalkin!

Second witch:
Paddock calls.

Third witch:
Anon.

All:
Fair is foul, and foul is fair:
Hover through the fog and filthy air.

Bully

You make me feel
So scared and small
The words that wound
The names you call

You make me feel
Like a piece of dirt
Your eyes that sting
Your looks that hurt

You make me feel
That I don't belong
What did I do
That was so wrong?

You make me feel
In a world apart
You took my soul
Ripped out my heart

But I can grow
I can be strong
I can be different
Yet still belong

Yes I can hold
My head up high
Smile deep inside
Then walk on by

Because I know
That bullying is wrong
So I'll stand up tall
I'll be proud and strong

Because I know
That what bullies do
Is because they hurt
Just like me and you.

© Sue Cowley 2007

Can You Keep a Secret?

Characters:
Charlie – nervous, jumpy
Sam – the leader
Jo – young, shy

Blackout. Curtains open. A single spotlight comes up on the three characters, crouched on the floor, looking down at a large package.

Charlie:	I'm scared, Sam.
Sam:	You're always scared, Charlie.
Jo:	Yeah, but this time there's a good reason.
Sam:	Oh shut up, Jo, you're not making things any better.
Charlie:	What are we going to do, Sam? About . . . you know . . . that . . . thing *[points at the bundle]*.
Sam:	How should I know? It's your fault, Charlie.
Charlie:	*[getting gradually more worked up]* That's not fair. It was an accident. You saw what happened. You were both there with me. That means it's your fault as much as mine.
Sam:	Look. We need to think straight. Work out what to do next. Get our story straight in case anyone asks about . . .
Charlie:	*[suddenly noticing the audience]* Hey! Look! What are they doing here? They're all staring at us. Listening to us. They must know about . . .
Jo:	*[looks up at audience too]* Look, Sam, look. Charlie's right. There's a load of people out there. Watching us. They must have seen us . . .
Sam:	*[standing up]* Don't be pathetic, you two. There's no way they could know. And as long as you keep quiet about it, no one's ever going to find out. You *are* going to keep quiet, aren't you? You *can* keep a secret, can't you?
Charlie:	Of course we can, Sam. We're not stupid.

Jo: But what are we going to do about . . . about that *[points at the bundle on the floor]*.

Sam: We'll just have to get rid of it. You know, like they do in the movies. Dump it some place. Somewhere it'll never be found. Chuck it in the canal. I dunno.

Jo: But it's too heavy, Sam. We'll never be able to move it.

Charlie: *[points at the audience]* And they're watching! We've got all these witnesses. What if they tell someone? Like the police?

Sam: We'll just have to hope that they can keep a secret.

Jo: Why don't we ask them to shut their eyes?

Charlie: Go on then.

Jo: Okay. *[to the audience]* Can you shut your eyes? Please?

Charlie: It didn't work. Look. They're all still watching.

Sam: I know!

Jo: What, Sam?

Sam: Let's turn out the lights.

Blackout

© Sue Cowley 2007

Index